The Rohingya Crisis

This book provides a history of the ethnic persecution of the Rohingyas in Myanmar and their disputed ethnic and national identity. It focuses on how the crisis has morphed into a geopolitical encounter among Bangladesh, China, India, and Myanmar. It further explores the moral, ethnographic, and public policy issues in the humanitarian response to the crisis of the Rohingya people.

The volume analyzes the question of citizenship for the Rohingyas by analyzing historical documents and interviews that chronicle the status and identity of the community and their past involvement in the government and politics of Myanmar. The authors focus specifically on the changing geopolitical context of state formation in South Asia and the tense relationships between Myanmar and its neighbors – Bangladesh, China, and India. The book examines the alliances and disputes in the South and Southeast Asia region, which are predicated on economic and strategic gains, and their impact on the Rohingya crisis. It also looks at the failure of bilateral and multilateral negotiations among these countries to adequately address or alleviate the plight of the stateless Rohingyas.

This volume will be of great interest to scholars and researchers of international studies, peace, human rights and conflict studies, sociology, ethnic studies, border studies, migration and diaspora studies, discrimination and exclusion studies, public policy, and Asian studies. It will also be useful for professionals working in the media, nongovernmental organizations (NGOs), think tanks, and policy makers, as well as general readers interested in the history of the persecution of the Rohingya people.

Norman K. Swazo is Professor of Philosophy and Director of the Office of Research at North South University, Dhaka, Bangladesh. He specializes in ethics in international affairs, recent European philosophy, biomedical ethics, and philosophy of religion. He is the author of numerous journal articles in these areas of research and the author of several books, including *Crisis Theory and World Order: Heideggerian Reflections*; *Destroying Idols: Revisioning* the Meaning of "God"; and *Heidegger's Entscheidung: "Decision" between "Fate" and "Destiny"*. He is the editor of *Contemporary Moral Philosophy and Applied Ethics: An Anthology* and contributing author to H. Bashir et al.'s *Co-Existing in a Globalized World: Key Themes in Inter-professional Ethics*.

Sk. Tawfique M. Haque is Professor and Chair of the Department of Political Science and Sociology of North South University (NSU), Bangladesh. He is also working as the director of the South Asian Institute of Policy and Governance (SIPG) at NSU. Professor Haque has experience in university teaching with more than 18 years of undergraduate- and postgraduate-level teaching in Norway, Sri Lanka, Bangladesh, Bhutan, and Nepal. He has published three books, ten book chapters from reputed international publishing houses, and more than 20 scientific research papers in national and international research journals in the fields of administrative culture, models of governance, NGO accountability, local civil society, globalization, and geopolitical issues.

Md. Mahbubul Haque is currently working at the Faculty of Law and International Relations in University Sultan Zainal Abidin (UNISZA) Malaysia. Of Bangladeshi origin, Mahbub conducted research with international nongovernmental organizations (INGOs) and NGOs in Bangladesh, Myanmar, Thailand, Indonesia, and Malaysia. He obtained a master's of arts in history from Dhaka University, Bangladesh, and a master's of arts in human rights from Mahidol University, Thailand. Later, in 2014, he obtained a PhD in human rights and peace studies from the same institute in Thailand. Mahbub has received scholarships from the Swedish International Development Cooperation Agency (SIDA). He has published numerous articles in internationally recognized academic journals and the 2019 book *Rohingya Survivors: Regional Security Implication of Gender Based Violence*.

Tasmia Nower is Lecturer at North South University (NSU), Bangladesh. Prior to joining NSU, she worked for FWCO Management Consultants as a researcher in Vancouver, Canada, for a broad range of projects with clients including Justice Canada and Health Canada. Previously, she worked on foreign aid and development projects for KfW German Development Bank and the United Nations Development Program–Bangladesh. Tasmia obtained her MA in international studies from Simon Fraser University in Canada and her bachelor's in international relations from Quest University Canada. Her MA thesis, "Sectarianism or Geopolitics? Framing the 2011 Syrian Conflict", explores the sectarian dynamic of the Syrian conflict. Before Canada, she lived in Japan and the United States.

The Rohingya Crisis
A Moral, Ethnographic, and Policy Assessment

Norman K. Swazo, Sk. Tawfique
M. Haque, Md. Mahbubul Haque,
and Tasmia Nower

LONDON AND NEW YORK

First published 2021
by Routledge
2 Park Square, Milton Park, Abingdon, Oxon OX14 4RN

and by Routledge
52 Vanderbilt Avenue, New York, NY 10017

Routledge is an imprint of the Taylor & Francis Group, an informa business

© 2021 South Asian Institute of Policy and Governance

The right of South Asian Institute of Policy and Governance to be identified as authors of this work has been asserted by them in accordance with sections 77 and 78 of the Copyright, Designs and Patents Act 1988.

All rights reserved. No part of this book may be reprinted or reproduced or utilised in any form or by any electronic, mechanical, or other means, now known or hereafter invented, including photocopying and recording, or in any information storage or retrieval system, without permission in writing from the publishers.

Trademark notice: Product or corporate names may be trademarks or registered trademarks, and are used only for identification and explanation without intent to infringe.

British Library Cataloguing-in-Publication Data
A catalogue record for this book is available from the British Library

Library of Congress Cataloging-in-Publication Data
A catalog record for this book has been requested

ISBN: 978-0-367-34133-6 (hbk)
ISBN: 978-0-429-32410-9 (ebk)
ISBN: 978-0-367-56925-9
Typeset in Times New Roman
by Apex CoVantage, LLC

Dedicated to the Rohingya people and their right to both self-identity and a homeland

Contents

List of photos viii
Foreword ix

1 The Rohingya crisis: a moral-philosophical assessment 1
   NORMAN K. SWAZO

2 The Rohingya crisis and geopolitics: a public
   policy conundrum 34
   SK. TAWFIQUE M. HAQUE AND TASMIA NOWER

3 A future for the Rohingya in Myanmar 52
   MD. MAHBUBUL HAQUE

   Index 79

Photos

3.1 Displaced Rohingya temporary shelters made from
 bamboo cane and filthy plastic, Cox's Bazar, Bangladesh 54
3.2 Rohingya education center in Terengganu State, Malaysia 57
3.3 Rohingya gathering after Friday prayer in Bangkok, Thailand 65
3.4 Displaced Rohingya shelter in Cox's Bazar, Bangladesh 69

Foreword

The Rohingya crisis has been a subject of discourse and debates for decades without any concrete outcome and solution. Knowing the subject at close range, I would definitely say the authors of this volume have achieved their objectives. They present a fair and balanced portrayal on the complexities, the intertwining issues, the problems, and the challenges of the crisis that affects the Rohingya, Myanmar, and Bangladesh.

The authors are well qualified to write on the subject. They have carried out extensive research to present their insights, ideas, and thoughts eloquently on various perspectives, covering the issues of ethno-religious nationalism of Buddhist Myanmar; providing philosophical, legal, moral, geopolitical, and socio-cultural arguments; and finally asking the questions on the future of the Rohingya in Myanmar. As a result, this book is of immediate relevance for the stakeholders in any discussion of the unresolved crisis. It is an excellent book for academics, policy makers, and students to read.

Dr. Syed Hamid Albar
Former Foreign Minister of Malaysia

1 The Rohingya crisis
A moral-philosophical assessment

Norman K. Swazo

It is a lamentable fact that the dire situation of "stateless" refugees has been exacerbated in the current century consequent to armed conflict and religious violence, even as it is clear responses to the refugee crisis internationally have their philosophical impetus in differing conceptions of moral duty, for example, communitarianism and liberalism (Papazoglou, 2019). Alexis Papazoglou describes the difference in conception of political responsibility thus:

> communitarianism . . . sees people's identities and value as intrinsically linked to their political community, political justice therefore rooted in and confined to that specific community, and liberalism, which recognizes universal human rights, and sees our political responsibilities extending beyond our narrow ethnic or political group to all human beings.

How to respond to the violence refugees experience clearly is grounded in these two conceptions of political responsibility and their associated moral presuppositions. Hence, what is deemed feasibly efficacious political intervention is unclear and, more often than not, relative to the context of the philosophical ground appropriated. Yet, the reality is that whatever the political concepts, the refugee finds himself and herself in a no-man's land of continuing uncertainty that no citizen ever appreciates fully – especially given the refugees' manifestations in the faces of desperate women, children, and the elderly. We can be instructed in this situation by political scientist Michael Dillon, who argued before the turn of the century that:

- The refugee is a scandal for philosophy in that the refugee recalls the radical instability of meaning and the incalculability of the human.

- The refugee is a scandal for politics also, however, in that the advent of the refugee is always a reproach to the formation of the political order or subjectivity which necessarily gives rise to the refugee.
- The scandal is intensified for any politics of identity which presupposes that the goal of politics is the realization of sovereign identity.

(Dillon, 1998)

Dillon offers here three propositions troubling for moral philosophers, political scientists, and policy makers who have to consider the practical options that sovereign states face when confronted with a refugee crisis. This is so for contemporary Myanmar, evident in the plight of the self-identifying Rohingya people, over 1 million of whom have fled their former "home" in the northern Rakhine state in the west of Myanmar in 1978, 1991, 1992, 2012, 2017–2018, and continuing into early 2019, only to suffer as stateless refugees in the neighboring country of Bangladesh and elsewhere in South Asia despite international calls for repatriation and guarantees of security of person and property.[1] There is no doubt that the Rohingya are refugees according to the definition given in the UN Convention Relating to the Status of Refugees, that is, "someone who is unable or unwilling to return to their country of origin owing to a well-founded fear of being persecuted for reasons of race, religion, nationality, membership of a particular social group, or political opinion" (UNHCR, 2010). There is no doubt, further, that they are a stigmatized people within Myanmar. As such, it is important to remember that "[a]lthough stigma is conceptualized as a personal mark or attribute . . . it is a social product, the fruit of structural conditions and power relationships established in societies" (UNHCR, 2010)[2] – which is the case for Rohingya both internal and external to Myanmar's Rakhine state, the locus of ongoing ethnic hostilities. The fact is that the structural conditions and power relationships related to ethnic identity and citizenship in Myanmar produce the stigmatization that officially excludes this ethnic group from the basic rights and fundamental freedoms of recognized citizens. From the perspective of refugee rights, it is troubling that the stigma is inevitably exported as host countries likewise remain unclear as to the moral legitimacy of the Rohingya ethnic identity. Such governmental doubt thereby adds unwittingly to sustained discrimination and diminution of their human dignity and the respect for persons the Rohingya should enjoy irrespective of the "imaginary geography"[3] of historically inconstant nation-state borders in South Asia. For the Burmese Buddhist majority, the Rohingya are "Bengalis", whereas for the Bangladesh government the Rohingya are "Myanmar nationals", although international law protects refugees from being rendered stateless whether by the country of origin or the host country. The Rohingya are in this case in a particularly ambiguous and precarious situation of loss of political, civil, social, economic, and cultural rights that the international community recognizes as *inviolable fundamental human rights* (i.e., in the International Covenant on Civil and Political Rights and the International Covenant on Economic, Social, and Cultural Rights).

According to estimates, more than 3,000 hectares of land in southeast Bangladesh (Cox's Bazar) have been converted to temporary shelter and emergency humanitarian modalities for more than 900,000 refugees, creating environmental, disaster preparedness, and management problems for the Bangladesh government and international aid agencies. As of March 2019, some 1.3 million people were targeted for health assistance, including large-scale vaccinations and disease surveillance, with varicella and acute watery diarrhea prominent morbidity concerns.[4] Of major import in this population displacement is the prospect of the spread of drug-resistant malaria, consequential for both the refugees and the Bangladeshi population in general (ICDDRB, 2018). Such is the pressing humanitarian concern for the Rohingya currently in Bangladesh, consistent with expectations deriving from liberal and universalist principles. But, there is also the linked moral obligation to "future generations" of present refugees, including those born in the camps who may be castigated and refused nationality and citizenship. The Rohingya have no realistic sense of homeland past, present, or future so long as the Government of Myanmar sustains its communitarian perspective, interpreted as being responsive to its own national duty and loyalty to Burma's traditional Buddhist majority. As in other cases of refugee flight, the Rohingya can all too easily become another group of "forgotten refugees" on the world stage of global migration (one need recall here only the long-standing dispute between Morocco and the Polisario Front over the status of the Western Sahara and the right of the Saharawi people to national liberation) (UNESCO, 2017; Swazo, 2007).

The Third Committee (Social, Humanitarian, and Cultural) of the UN General Assembly, acting on November 16, 2018, approved a draft resolution introduced by Turkey on behalf of the Organization of Islamic Cooperation (OIC) condemning all rights violations in Myanmar and expressing concern for "the gravest crimes under international law" (UNGA, 2018).[5] More recently, at its meeting in Abu Dhabi, the OIC adopted a resolution championed by Gambia to involve the International Court of Justice in arbitrating the dispute with a view to settling the question of the legal rights of the Rohingya (OIC Okays Legal Action Against Myanmar, 2019).[6] Rejecting the resolution of November 2018 as "one-sided, biased, and hopelessly unconstructive", the Government of Myanmar decried the lack of attention to "the threat of terrorism" with the dubious claim that the Arakan Rohingya Salvation Army (ARSA) is linked to ISIL/Da'esh (the Islamic State of Iraq and Syria). The representative of Bangladesh spoke to the need for Myanmar to guarantee "a pathway to citizenship and land ownership" for the Rohingya. Yet, the fact is that the history of refugees does not bode well for secure repatriation, which poses an ethical dilemma for host countries and international governmental and non-governmental organizations (NGOs), as Mollie Gerver has reported (Gerver, 2018a; 2018b).[7]

The Government of Myanmar seeks to justify its security operations as a "counterinsurgency" action, although international observers dispute this to be a mere rationalization for persecution ("by law, by practice, and by policy") that amounts to ethnic cleansing and genocide (Berkley Forum, 2017).[8] In a statement issued on May 15, 2018, from the President's Office of the Government of Myanmar, Myanmar's UN ambassador was cited for remarks made at the UN Security Council briefing held on May 14, 2018 (President's Office, 2018). In that statement, Ambassador Hau Do Suan summarized the government's position on the Myanmar issue. He stated that "no violations of human rights will be condoned" but that the government requires any and all allegations to be "supported by evidence" in contrast to narratives (to warrant investigation and lawful remedy) and supports a "safe, dignified and voluntary return of the displaced persons", including repatriation "to their villages" in Rakhine state. But, he added, this must be "in accordance with the bilateral agreements" concluded with Bangladesh that assure proper verification procedures (including appropriate government forms, signatures, fingerprints, photographs, and assurance of consent to return, thus documentation to assure they were previously resident in Rakhine state). The mounting evidence, however, is that whatever repatriation is to occur will not be to former villages in Rakhine but instead to Rohingya "camps" segregated from Buddhist nationals, with many Buddhists being allowed relocation to Rakhine state to prevent the return of the Rohingya to their village homes, and that mitigates against any militant Rohingya intention to seek political autonomy in Rakhine (McPherson, Lewis, Aung, Naing, & Siddiqui, 2018).

The ambassador also claimed, "The root cause of the latest crisis and the brutal killings and atrocity committed by the terrorists on innocent ethnic Hindu, Rakhine Buddhists and other minority tribes had been ignored by the western media" in favor of "incessant sensational argument of Muslim victimhood narratives". Hence, the Government of Myanmar expects that Islamic terrorists "must also be held accountable for atrocities committed against civilian population in Rakhine". At the same time, government authorities have expressed their motivations, for example, Myanmar's Minister for Religious Affairs and Culture, Thura Aung Ko, expressing fear of a demographic transition as the Muslim birth rate exceeds that of the current

Buddhist majority and thereby threatens the Buddhist-centric political culture of the country (Sumon, 2018).

Accordingly, in his statement of October 24, 2018, before the UN Security Council, Ambassador Suan reiterated that Myanmar "categorically rejects inference of 'genocidal intent' on the legitimate counter terrorist actions by the security forces in Rakhine", especially inasmuch as the allegation of such intent "is made on unverified circumstantial evidences which [have] no sound legal proof" (Government of Myanmar, 2018). As part of the government's efforts to respond to counterinsurgency, approximately 240,000 Rohingya remain in Rakhine with their movement restricted by military/security forces with some 130,000 located in government "camps" set up in 2012 (Wright & Rivers, 2018). The Rohingya situation is also being complicated by armed conflict between Buddhist armed groups (Arakan Army) and Myanmar military forces as the former seek greater local autonomy ("Thousands Flee . . .", 2019). Some of this group has also crossed into Bangladesh, causing the government to once again take action to seal its border against further migration of refugees ("Bangladesh Seals Off Border . . .", 2019).

That said, however, for its part the Bangladesh government identifies the Rohingya as "forcibly displaced Myanmar nationals", even as it has moved to provide basic humanitarian support for them in the southeast of the country. The Bangladesh government has opined that "bilateral solutions" have been for the most part "largely unproductive", Bangladesh's foreign secretary, for example, stating that the Government of Myanmar is "not very sincere about their commitments" (XChange Foundation, 2018).[9] Foremost at issue here is the question of citizenship if the Rohingya are indeed properly to be denominated "Myanmar nationals". Despite protests to the contrary by the authorities in Myanmar, other prominent human rights groups such as the Public International Law and Policy Group (PILPG) have argued credibly that Myanmar security forces are guilty of crimes against humanity, war crimes, and genocide (Public International Law & Policy Group, 2018).[10] The European Union has issued a formal resolution to have the UN Security Council refer the Rohingya matter to the International Criminal Court, condemning "systematic attacks" against the Rohingya not only in Rakhine state but also in Kachin and Shan states (European Parliament, 2019).[11] Further crimes are alleged to be committed in trafficking of Rohingya women to China in forced marriage arrangements. The operational burden on the Bangladesh government is quite high, with some US$920 million sought by the Joint Response Team in February 2019 to provide ongoing care to the Rohingya in southeast Bangladesh ("Rohingya Refugees . . .", 2019).

Without doubt, here we find a situation of *radical instability of meaning*, which Dillon understands as discoverable in various refugee situations.

How so? Neil MacGregor (2017) clarifies the pertinent point. He reminds that we all have a "compelling need . . . for stories that give shape and significance to our individual lives" and that "religious stories" in particular are strategically important to "communal survival", what as such are *not truly empirically warranted explanations* that address "the conundrums of life and death" but, instead, stories that offer *meaning* to our lives. Buddhism and Islam provide meaning to Buddhists and Muslims, respectively, through such stories, even as these narratives are expressions of *doctrinal beliefs* that contribute to ethnic identity and, thereby, to sociopolitical tensions among ethnic groups. MacGregor is reminiscent of French sociologist Émile Durkheim's observations about the significance of narratives: "[w]e are, as a group, the stories we tell about ourselves. If, for whatever reason, we lose or forget those narratives, we collectively no longer exist". Such "constructed meaning" is part of the politics of identity that continuously evolves in the setting of the modern nation-state. But, constructions of meaning can be deceptive and distracting from reality. As the philosopher of science Alex Rosenberg has argued, we can become victims of narratives, "especially narrative history" that is "flawed" as a tool of knowledge, that is, "historical narratives" that "seduce" us "into thinking [we] really understand what's going on and why things happened" but all of which amounts to "a false account" of history (Chen, 2018; Rosenberg, 2018).

The politics of identity and the problem of disputed historical narratives are front and center in the Rohingya crisis in Myanmar because it is unclear (1) who are the Rohingya, really, assuming a distinction of constructed historical narrative and a "true" explanatory account?; (2) who counts as a legitimate citizen, according to Myanmar's sovereign authority, stipulated in the 1982 Citizenship Act? (Burma Citizenship Law, 2018);[12] (3) what ethnicities are legally identified and welcome today, whatever the history of their pre- or post-colonial presence in the territory of present-day Myanmar?; and (4) what religious convictions are to be tolerated or, alternatively, depreciated, according to sectarian, communalist dispositions? The latter question is at the heart of a moral dilemma, evident from the time of "extremely violent Buddhist-Muslim clashes of 1942" in Myanmar, clashes that "created wounds that never healed and cemented the division between Buddhist and Muslim communities in northern Rakhine" and that did not settle outstanding claims of "territorial dispossession" (Leider, 2013). Who "the dispossessed" are in Myanmar is a complex question when evaluated in the context of ambiguous historical narratives about ethnic identity. Thus, even as it may be argued that "identity is personal" in the sense of a right to self-identification, that is, according to extant human rights law, nonetheless, as Yussef AlTamimi remarks, the fact is that identity is "simultaneously constituted and shaped by overarching power mechanisms" (AlTamimi, 2018).

For example, AlTamimi observes, in case law the European Court of Human Rights

> tends to construct a notion of identity that abides by a state's accepted norms and assesses the applicant's claim through that construct. Identity features that deviate from the state's conventional identity are considered excesses of identity, which have to be accommodated into the state system. At times, this may obstruct the recognition of certain identity features.

The same sort of reasoning may be employed in the case of the principal question at issue concerning the citizenship status of the Rohingya, regardless of whether ethnocentric or religio-centric factors are contributing variables. The fact is, nonetheless, that whatever the stipulation of a right to identity, that in and of itself does not translate automatically into an acknowledged duty to heed and not violate that right. One may ask, consistent with due legal process, whether a Rohingya, considered severally, has a right to citizenship, such as he or she demands. One may ask, further to that question, whether – *assuming* such a right and *claiming* the right has been violated – the laws of Myanmar (either constitutional or statutory) afford a Rohingya (severally) a remedy of justice. Finally, moreover, if the laws of Myanmar do provide for legal remedy, then one may query which judicial institution or national authority is properly to issue the remedy prescribed by law or otherwise according to some authoritative discretionary judgment that carries the force of law.

Even so, as Michael Jerryson has argued, the fact is that "[r]eligion is the rhetorical means of persecuting and targeting the Rohingya" (Jerryson, 2017). He cites a *Guardian* interview with the Burmese Buddhist monk U Rarzar (a member of the Association for the Protection of Race and Religion) who is quoted to say, "The Muslims have started a jihad. The Muslims, they murdered one of our Buddhist monks. They slaughtered him. Poured petro on him and burned him alive. Their acts of terror are causing conflict in our country". Jerryson rightly observes that the language here, the narration, is prejudicially loaded – a "threat is identified through religious language – jihad and Muslim identity". On this view, it is not merely the Rohingya but all Muslims who are an "existential" threat to traditionally Burmese Buddhist society despite allowances for the presence of Chinese Muslims (the Panthays) and others known as the Kamein. Yet, Myanmar has proposed to be a fledgling democracy since the elections of 2015, in which case there should be reasonable accommodation of ethnic diversity without complicity in actions amounting to ethnic cleansing or genocide. Jerryson writes elsewhere that even so, "[a]s perpetrators of violence rarely locate themselves as aggressors or see themselves as deficient in moral justifications", nonetheless the fact is that "Buddhists see intentionality as influential in the ethics of such acts", in which case we should disabuse ourselves of "the ahistorical myth that Buddhists are wholly peaceful" (Jerryson, 2015).

Tina Mumford (2017) concurs with Jerryson's remarks: religion in Myanmar is "an agent of social cleavage" with societal actors in Myanmar "deliberately and maliciously" tapping into "this inherent divisiveness to advance agenda that are religo-centric and ethnocentric". Such an agenda conduces to "Burmese society's outward lack of empathy for the slaughter of their fellow humans". Hence, any reasonable response to the crisis requires attention to the role of religion, Mumford argues, problematic here in that the conflict centers on Myanmar's Buddhist society and its fear of Islamization of the country, whether through a Muslim *jihād* or through a demographic transition through growth in the Muslim population within the country. Katherine Marshall concurs with Mumford's observations, taking note of violence that relates to "religious teachings and leadership" (Marshall, 2017). Her question is: "can appeals to religious beliefs and institutions and to the peacebuilding mission of so many religious traditions help towards a solution?"

Marshall accounts for the problem of historical narrative likewise, "fabled political, economic, and social factors, magnified by long historic resentments", and thus far there is no evidence of a prospective "appeal. . . [to] a shared call to compassion", especially when perpetrators in the military/security forces are nominally Buddhist and enforcing a supposed counter-insurgency action supported by majority Buddhist sentiment in the country. Here there remains an unsettled question whether this narrative is merely pretext for a more geopolitical issue concerning bilateral international relations (e.g., with China) in the use of the Rakhine territory for economic motivations. It is no wonder, then, that the international community is being awakened to the falsity of the generalized narrative of Buddhist compassion. As Maung Zarni remarks, "I think we should stop romanticizing Buddhism and Buddhists as more peaceful than any other people. . . . There is a romanticized, rosy, orientalised [perception] of Buddhism among the English speaking population around the world and other non-English speakers as well . . . but that's just so false" – given that Buddhism has been used and abused "as a political ideology dating back thousands of years and was as susceptible to political manipulation in the same way as Christianity, Islam, Hinduism, and Judaism" (Chang, Yasin, Dwip, Kenyon, & Lederer, 2017). Charles Haviland (2015) opines consonantly, speaking of the "darker side of

Buddhism" present in recent times in ethnic conflict in Sri Lanka as well as Myanmar, in Sri Lanka perpetrated by the "hardline Buddhist organisation, the Bodu Bala Sena or Buddhist Power Force (BBS)". The Buddhists here are at once religio-centric and ethnocentric, "three quarters" of the population of Sri Lanka being "ethnically Sinhalese", in which case unsurprisingly the Buddhist monk Galagoda Aththe Gsanasara Thero argues, "This country belongs to the Sinhalese, and it is the Sinhalese who built up its civilization, culture and settlements" (Haviland, 2015) – a sentiment that resonates as the Burmese Buddhists seek to preserve their ethnic prerogatives against what they perceive to be Muslim encroachment.

Of course, as the foregoing observations inform us, there is, as Akhilesh Pillamarri (2017) reminds, "a long and complicated history" of the interaction of Buddhism and Islam in Asia. This includes conflict in shared spaces – "Rakhine state in Myanmar, southern Thailand, Sri Lanka, and Ladakh, the eastern part of the Indian state of Jammu and Kashmir". In all these places foremost at issue is fear of a demographic transition and loss of traditional culture, given that the historical record shows "[o]ften, the arrival of Islam went hand-in-hand with the destruction of Buddhism". In the case of Myanmar, "[i]f all Rohingya refugees were to be repatriated to Rakhine . . . they would outnumber the local Buddhist Rakhine people" (Pillamarri, 2017), a fact that generates political tensions and sundry problems in local governance, with Buddhists feeling themselves "under siege" and their future as an ethnic and religious majority in jeopardy, hence their xenophobia that is specifically Islamophobic.

Problematic here is the convergence of religious identity and national identity with the violence that thereby erupts from these two ideological appeals in combination (Wade, 2017). As Francis Wade puts it, "The majority of people in Myanmar appear to see the Rohingya as crusading Islamizers bent on dislodging Buddhism from its central position in society. This, therefore, makes them a greater menace to the young democracy than an invigorated military" (Wade, 2017). Hence, within Myanmar there is a "powerful Buddhist national lobby that believes human rights should be conferred selectively", consistent with the ethnic legitimacy recognized by the state.

Viewed from the perspective of anthropology of religion, at issue here is the combination of the *Theravada* branch of Buddhism in its linkage to Buddhist nationalism in many countries in South and Southeast Asia. Charles Keyes (2016), for example, points to a contemporary conundrum inasmuch as "Buddhists from the very beginning of the religion have had to engage rather than shun politics", the engagement with Muslims unavoidably part of the political past and present. Francis Brassard (2006) has discussed the relation between Buddhist theory and practice, accounting for both the possibility and the actuality of violence, direct or indirect, therein. He examines how "ideas that are primarily designed to bring about a spiritual experience, may exert an influence on the values of a society to the point that some of its members are discriminated against or even oppressed"; that is, a "good idea" can have "negative consequences". Brassard's (2006) premise is that "[i]f a spiritual or religious idea can be used to create social differences, then one is not very far from having a society that discriminates, and even oppresses some of its members on the basis of such an idea". In a situation of perceived existential threat from Islam, such as one finds among nationalist and ethnocentric Buddhists in Myanmar, then manifest differences in ethnic identity and allowances for citizenship lead inevitably to discrimination and oppression as occurs with the persecution of the Rohingya. The "irony" between theory and practice is clear: "an idea expressly prohibiting violence may have been the cause or the justification of a social structure that promotes discrimination and violence". That is, "as soon as there is a dominant system of values" – as in Buddhist values complicated by ethnic identity – "that, on the one hand promotes certain members of that society and, on the other hand, excludes or disenfranchises other members, some degree of violence is exerted" (Brassard, 2006).

In keeping with this argument, Christoph Kleine (2006) takes into account that one can speak meaningfully of "evil monks" who have "good intentions", that is, that Buddhist monastic violence has its doctrinal basis. This is so for "organized and institutionalized violence" that deviates "from the Buddha's original intention" – the traditional "monastic code" including the killing of human beings among the "major offenses". Yet, the fact is that "religious people modify their beliefs and doctrines, moral codes, and practices". Even then, as Kleine (2006) observes, the Mahayanistic moral code (as in the case of Buddhist Japan) "laid more emphasis on a given person's intention and mental attitude than on his actions". Thus, the argument holds that even as "a bodhisattva was entitled to break minor rules if the breaking of the rule benefited others and was performed with an irreproachable (*nirvadya*) motive", so "the breaking of major rules . . . was tolerable, nay expected, if performed on the basis of the three supreme qualities of a bodhisattva: (1) skill in means (*upāya-kauśalya*), (2) insight (*prajñā*), and (3) compassion (*karuṇā*)", the latter assuming compassion for the welfare of others (Kleine, 2006).

In the case of Burmese Buddhist monks, their compassion is directed at the welfare of Buddhist nationals in Myanmar who, at least in their perception if not in fact, are threatened by Muslim *jihād* and a demographic transition as Muslims begin to outnumber confessant Buddhists, such as in Rakhine. On this view, the Buddhist exercises violence "with merit". Yet, there is a further, more fundamental, feature of Buddhist metaphysics that enables the murder of human beings. Consider the following argument as Kleine (2006) cites it:

> [i]f there are no beings then there is no offense of killing either. Because there is no offense of killing there is no upholding of precepts either. Also, when one deeply enters into the contemplation [of the five aggregates, *skandhas*], one analyzes and realizes that they are empty, like something seen in a dream, and like images in a mirror. If one kills something seen in a dream or an image in a mirror there is no killing offense committed. One kills the empty marks [*śūnyatānimitta*] of the five aggregates. Beings are just the same as this.

Westerners not aware of such Buddhist metaphysical reasoning clearly are not in a position to determine how a Buddhist may murder and find merit in it consistent with both the moral code and Buddhist metaphysics. This is one element of Buddhist politics that is subject to critique when countered by international humanitarian law and the Western tradition of human rights. Despite such metaphysical arguments, there is the more practically grounded argument, vis-à-vis, that national governments seeking solidarity of the body politic readily appropriate religious traditions, as has happened in the case of Burma up to and including the present Government of Myanmar in its deference to institutionalized Theravada Buddhism and to the nationalist Buddhism supported by the Burmese people generally.

In the case of Myanmar, Keyes observes, the Buddhists have long defended their ethnic and politically defined prerogatives, having in the past practiced ethnic cleansing "by compelling a large percentage of the Indian population to leave the country". Myanmar continues to show through official actions that its religio-centric policies amount to support for a kind of "Buddhist fundamentalism" intentionally harnessing "'fundamental' aspects of Buddhism . . . for nationalist, xenophobic purposes", in which case there are those who argue that such political appropriation cannot be "true Buddhism" (Whitaker, 2017). That means here, of course, not true Theravada Buddhism, even as one such as the Dalai Lama, the exiled spiritual leader of the Mahayana branch of Buddhism in Tibet, has spoken against the hostilities targeting Muslims in Myanmar, although some argue he should be more outspoken in condemning these hostilities (Westcott & George, 2017).

The international community has reproached the Government of Myanmar for persecution of the Rohingya at the hands of its military and for causing a refugee problem as more than a million have fled into Bangladesh over a time frame of decades. Ethnic and religious tensions are manifestly evident as the Buddhist-majority country rejects the Rohingya for their ethnicity as "former Bengalis" (some will say former "Pakistanis from Chittagong" [Leider, 2013], meaning here "East Pakistani", thus what is currently Bangladesh) and for their religion as Muslims. Indeed, post-colonial Myanmar is particularly dominated by a starkly determinate sense of ethnicity. As Jacques P. Leider (2013) argues, if one accepts the underlying assumption that "cultural characteristics" are "markers of a fixed identity", then people can be "divided into essentialized ethnic categories", advancing thereby a "culturalist" and racial understanding of ethnic identity. In the case of Myanmar, Leider observes, this understanding has had the consequence of identification of some "135 ethnic groups, a list that reflects political choices based on ethnic, cultural and historical criteria". In and of themselves such criteria are perhaps innocuous, but such criteria become politically problematic when "groups are hierarchized" only to install some as "dominant and prominent" to the diminution or exclusion of others.

Most anthropologists today reject this culturalist understanding of ethnic identity for its essentialist doctrine. Leider (2013) reminds that "[a]nthropological research tells us that ethnic identity is not intrinsically given and fixed, but subject to change as much as society as a whole is nowhere fitting a once-for-all model". As a matter of the empirical data of anthropology, Leider (2013) adds, "Identities undergo transformation, as people migrate and adapt to new places, to socio-economic change and to cultural challenges". This scientific view contrasts to the political situation in Myanmar, where "ethnic identity is a fixed concept that defines the identity of the State and it is not seen as something that can be either questioned, changed or reinvented". Clearly, this political position is problematic for the prospect of coexistence of Buddhists and Muslims in Myanmar, especially in the case of the Muslim Rohingya of the northern Rakhine state, given that the sovereign authority of Myanmar does not legally accept the Rohingya claim to a legitimate presence in the country. Bangladesh Foreign Secretary Shahidul Haque comments on the narrative deployed by Myanmar authorities:

> They have a very good propaganda machine . . . using it against a particular community. . . . Some of the things that are being said are absolutely incorrect. Number 1: they think the Rohingyas are Bengalis from Bangladesh, that is the first narrative, so they should go back to Bangladesh. Second they are all terrorists. . . . The third narrative is that the sovereignty and security of Myanmar is at threat, so they have every right to deploy whatever they want to protect their sovereignty.
> (Dillabough-LeFebvre, 2018b)

Yet, one such as Anchalee Rütland opines that "[w]hat appears historically verified on the current state of research is the claim that Muslims had indeed settled in Arakan (now Rakhine) prior to the Burmese conquest in 1784. . . . In fact, the earliest historical sources mentioning Muslim settlers date back to the late 16th century and suggest that they had travelled on trading fleets from Bengal to Rakhine" (Rütland, 2017).[13]

Hence, the Government of Myanmar refuses to the Rohingya the right of citizenship even as it does not assure them of personal or collective security against communalist violence. If the Rohingya do not have a state-identified ethnic identity, if the very concept of Rohingya is contested for its legitimacy, as is currently the case, then they are considered first and foremost as "Bengalis", thus as illegal aliens having no legitimate right of residence. Despite the Constitution of 1948 guaranteeing liberty of belief, faith, and worship, the citizenship clause 11.iv stipulated restrictions that applied to the Rohingya, to wit:

> (iv) every person who was born in any of the territories which at the time of his birth was included within His Britannic Majesty's dominions and who has resided in any of the territories included within the Union for a period of not less than eight years in the ten years immediately preceding the date of the commencement of this Constitution or immediately preceding the 1st January 1942 and who intends to reside permanently therein and who signifies his election of citizenship of the Union in the manner and within the time prescribed by law, shall be a citizen of the Union.
> (The Constitution. . ., 2018)[14]

Although the Rohingya might have appealed to the authority of this provision in adjudicating the issue of citizenship, the subsequent constitutional reforms articulated in the Constitution adopted in May 2008 stipulate a commitment to "non-disintegration of the Union", hence the insistent clause 1.10 forbidding secession and section 1.40(c) authorizing the Defence Services to respond to any "state of emergency that could cause disintegration of the Union" (Myanmar Ministry, 2018). Sections 1.34 and 8.362 entitle citizens to free practice of religion but "subject to public order". Chapter 8.345 defines citizenship in a restrictive manner according to two qualifications: (1) a person of parents both of whom are nationals of the Republic of the Union of Myanmar and (2) a person who is already a citizen according to law on the day the Constitution was adopted. Technically, this excludes the Rohingya population insofar as they are not "nationals" in the legal sense stipulated.

Furthermore, with the creation of the Rohingya Solidarity Organization in 1982 as a "militant organization" seeking the creation of "an autonomous Arakan state uniting the Rohingyas of Burma and Bangladesh" and subsequent formations such as the Arakan Rohingya Union (formed "under the patronage of the Organization of the Islamic Conference"), the Government of Myanmar and the Buddhist majority stand definitively in opposition inasmuch as it portends secession (Leider, 2013). It is also reported, however, that "[u]ntil the military took over control in 1962, the Muslim population in Rakhine was not only socially better integrated, but also enjoyed the same civic rights as the Buddhist Rakhines" (Rütland, 2017). That said, it is important also to bear in mind that there is no uniformity of view among the Muslims in Rakhine. Leider (2013) reminds that "[m]iddle-class Rohingyas" have a "moderate discourse" that is "in striking contrast with the aggressive stance of certain Rohingya militants outside the country", these Muslims seeking "freedom of worship, guarantees against religious persecution and the same political and economic rights for Muslims as other communities in Burma".[15] Such is the confused politics of identity and the problematic features of a constructed historical narrative among the Rohingya internal and external to Myanmar.

Leider opines that if one accounts for "their modern origins", that is, since the 1950s, then "the Rohingyas are best defined as a political and militant movement", political and militant insofar as they have had as their aim "the creation of an autonomous Muslim zone" in Myanmar – hence eliciting the ire of the Buddhist majority. The politics of identity is at the heart of the current crisis such that it will not do merely to identify the Rohingya as victims and the Buddhists or government military as perpetrators, as Leider has argued. One must ask:

- does it matter – *culturally, politically, legally, morally* – that "the forefathers of the overwhelming majority of Muslims in Rakhine have migrated from Bengal to Rakhine" (Leider, 2013)?
- does it matter, similarly that "[d]uring the colonial period, most migrants came from Chittagong Division [of current Bangladesh]" (Leider, 2013)? If there is demonstrably historical veracity to these claims – that is, these are not mere statements of a convenient narrative – then it is neither "discriminatory" nor "derogatory" to assert, as many in Myanmar do, that the contemporary Muslim Rohingya are factually "Bengalis". This is so despite their claim to the ethnic identity of Rohingya that is more than a mere "political accommodation" or "linguistic habit" for a "politically correct" but factually problematic category in use.[16]
- does it matter that to the contrary, the Rohingya claim a descent, over centuries, from Arab and Persian traders, thus a residence in the territory for generations (Leider, 2013)?

- does it matter that some, like Andrew Selth, argue that most of the "Bengali Muslims" living in Arakan state and who self-identify as Rohingya "arrived with the British colonialists in the 19th and 20th centuries" – whether through deportation or resettlement as dictated by British rule or economic opportunity[17] – hence a migrant population who were never "naturally" Burmese or "culturally" an officially identified ethnic group within Burma (Leider, 2013)?
- does it matter, as a point of political fact, that "[u]nder the British administration between 1826 and 1937, there were no limits to Bengali migration to Rakhine as temporary workers and permanent settlers advanced the agricultural exploitation of the land" (Leider, 2013)?
- does it matter, further, as Azeem Ibrahim (2016) reminds, that Myanmar's "establishment narrative ignores the convenient reality that the territory occupied by historical Burmese state does not correspond neatly to the territory of Myanmar today: the modern province of Rakhine was only ever part of the earlier Burmese states for relatively brief periods of time", in which case there is no "perfect match between ethnic groups and political boundaries"?
- does it matter that the ethnic identities in present-day Myanmar are a function of cultural contact and convergence, such that "by the mid-1990s around one-third of the population of Myanmar was made up of ethnic groups distinct from the Burman majority" and that this "naturally reflected the history of interaction from China to the north, India to the west, Thailand and Laos to the east and Indonesia and Malaysia to the south" (Ibrahim, 2016)?

Depending on answers to these questions, one may presumably refer, therefore, to the conflict (since 1977–1978) as one between "Arakanese-Buddhists" and "Muslim-Bengalis", as did Klaus Fleischmann in his report of the initial refugee crisis at the time that entangled Burmese and Bangladeshi authorities as to appropriate policies of remediation and conflict resolution. On this view, the conflict is ethnic and religious in its origin, and the Arakanese Buddhists are a legitimate, officially recognized ethnic group seeking to obstruct any autonomous Muslim zone in Rakhine; that is the post-World War 2 goal of "illegal immigrants" who have no political/civil rights to demand anything like autonomy.

The issue here is at once legal and moral even as it is cultural and political. The basic *legal* claim from the government authorities is that the Rohingya are illegal immigrants, for example, from what was earlier East Pakistan (prior to 1971), now Bangladesh, hence the denomination "Bengali". They are not one of the officially recognized ethnic groups in Myanmar. As such, they have no rights of citizenship and are subject to the laws governing treatment of illegal aliens. The political dimension is further complicated by the fact that some "Arakanese Muslims" are not "Muslim nationalists", that is, they are not calling for the autonomous zone the latter do in identifying themselves as Rohingya and in spurring an ideological movement of "militant struggle" (Leider, 2013). Not all are in agreement with the militant goals of the *Aqa Mul Mujahidin* (the Arakan Rohingya Salvation Army, ARSA). The *moral* issue here is whether, despite the fact that the Rakhine Muslim group has no official recognition "within the nomenclature of Myanmar ethnicities", nonetheless the Government of Myanmar has *humanitarian obligations* toward this ethnic group, consistent with international humanitarian law and generally accepted human rights standards. Most who evaluate this question argue that the Government of Myanmar does have such moral obligations, even as they have a duty under international law not to take political or security actions that cause individuals otherwise resident within the national territory to become stateless.

Preliminary assessment of prohibited "atrocity crimes"

It is today clear that the international community has raised the question whether elements of the Government of Myanmar, the military specifically, have engaged in violations of humanitarian law and human rights through ongoing persecution of the Rohingya community. At issue definitively is whether this persecution amounts to (1) ethnic cleansing (U.S. Department of State, 2018),[18] (2) crimes against humanity and war crimes,[19] or (3) genocide (van Schaack, 2018a).[20] The Government of Bangladesh in particular is at the forefront of the quest for a just and peaceful resolution of the crisis.[21] It is reported that in an initial round of refugee movement, since 2015, "over 900,000 Rohingya have fled to southeastern Bangladesh alone, and more to other surrounding countries" (Noor, Thudi, Islam, & Forid, 2017). After so-called clearance operations conducted by the Myanmar military in August 2017, another 603,000 Rohingya reportedly fled to Bangladesh. At issue is whether the military of Myanmar, with the direct support or negligence of the Government of Myanmar, has committed crimes against humanity. If so, in the absence of national investigation and prosecution, the question now is whether this is a matter subject to the jurisdiction of the International Criminal Court (ICC).

Myanmar is not currently a State Party to the Rome Statute that established the ICC. Bangladesh, however, is a signatory State Party, having done so on March 23, 2010. Because Bangladesh bears the onus of the refugee influx, it has just cause to pursue remedy as it formulates and implements policy options in coordination with the international community through bilateral assistance and international governmental and NGO support and working with local civil society organizations. The government of Bangladesh, itself a lower middle-income country, has limited resources to respond to the influx of refugees, and is dependent on foreign humanitarian assistance even as it seeks repatriation of the Rohingya to Myanmar. Basic living needs are under threat, with the continuing congestion of refugees in the southeast of Bangladesh rife for a public health crisis where there is little primary medical care available, a lack of an adequate potable water supply and basic sanitation (hence the threat of diarrheal disease, cholera, typhoid, spread of communicable disease among unvaccinated children, etc.), not to mention inadequacy of food and cooking fuels (Ahmed et al., 2018; World Health Organization Weekly Situation Report #32, 2018). Because this is a Muslim group, many men practice polygamy, having large families, adding to problems of management of pregnancy and sanitary conditions for full-term births. Many young women among the Rohingya claim to be victims of rape by the Myanmar military forces, hence one of the elements of crimes against humanity.

The UN Security Council (UNSC) reviewed the situation in Myanmar at a meeting held on February 13, 2018, which was followed by another review on August 28, 2018 (UNSC, 2018). At the latter meeting, the UN secretary-general opined that "the massive refugee emergency" caused by exodus from Rakhine state "has become one of the world's worst humanitarian and human rights crises". To the degree the Myanmar military has responded to insurgent attacks from militant Rohingya, the secretary-general argued that "such attacks could never justify the disproportionate use of force against civilian populations". Relevant local and international authorities agreed on a "framework for cooperation to create the conditions for the voluntary, safe, dignified and sustainable repatriation of refugees from Bangladesh" (UNSC, 2018).[22] In addition to the refugee issue, there remains concern for persecution and discrimination of the Rohingya who remain in Myanmar, some 130,000 "confined in camps" and restricted as to the basic rights essential to a sustained livelihood.

The factual basis for UNSC review is the "Report of the Independent International Fact-Finding Mission on Myanmar", issued by the Human Rights Council on August 24, 2018 (Human Rights Council, 2018).[23] Section VI of this report concerns crimes under international law, including here genocide, crimes against humanity, and war crimes, the mission concluding that there are "reasonable grounds that serious crimes under international law have been committed that warrant criminal investigation and prosecution".[24] The mission reports that Myanmar security forces (i.e., the Tatmadaw) have committed prohibited acts falling under the definition of genocide, including (1) killing, (2) causing serious bodily or mental harm, (3) inflicting conditions of life calculated to bring about the destruction of the group in whole or in part, and (4) imposing measures intending to prevent births. At issue here is whether these actions are merely incidental to security force operations or there is basis for "reasonable inference" of "genocidal intent". The mission argues that genocidal intent is present, manifest in "oppressive context", "hate rhetoric", "specific utterances of commanders and direct perpetrators", "exclusionary policies" contributing to an alteration of "the demographic composition of Rakhine State", "the level of organization indicating a plan for destruction", and "extreme scale and brutality of the violence".[25]

The mission report argues there is evidence of crimes against humanity consistent with that definition, including murder, imprisonment, enforced disappearance, torture, rape, sexual slavery, and so on, manifested further in "elements of extermination and deportation" of the Rohingya population. Whether there are war crimes strictly defined is not immediately evident, depending on how the "non-international armed conflicts" in Rakhine state are evaluated. There are "non-State armed groups" (e.g., the Buddhist Rakhine, the United Wa State Army) that contribute to prohibited acts, the mission opining that "individual criminal liability" seemingly extends "beyond individual perpetrators, to their hierarchical commanders".[26] Accordingly, the mission calls for "accountability in line with recognized international norms and standards". Whether that be accountability conducted by due process of law nationally or through international institutions is a matter of contention as to appropriate jurisdiction, especially because the Government of Myanmar and civilian authorities have not met their responsibility to protect the civilian population and have engaged in obstructive actions to thwart investigation into acts prohibited under international law.

The mission argues that whereas "Myanmar authorities have created ad hoc inquiry commissions and boards", (1) "[n]one meets the standard of an impartial, independent, effective and thorough human rights investigation" and (2) "none has led to any prosecution for gross human rights violations and redress for victims".[27] Furthermore, "military courts" subject to the authority of the Tatmadaw "are inadequate forums to deal with large-scale human rights violations perpetrated by the military" even as civilian courts are "not independent" and lack "capacity to respect fair trial standards". These claims are pertinent in light of prior ICC actions. In the Kenyatta Appeal Judgment of August 30, 2011, for example, the chamber was clear that mere assertion of preparations for investigation is insufficient. Instead, the state must "provide the Court with evidence of a sufficient degree of specificity and probative value that demonstrates that it is indeed investigating the case". The chamber further clarified that "determining the existence of an investigation" is different from a state's being "unwillingly or unable genuinely to carry out the investigation or prosecution" ("Decision . . .", 2011). These same criteria apply in the case of Myanmar if it wishes the ICC to defer to its national jurisdiction in view of adherence to the principle of complementarity. That there is inadequate redress is evident from the unsolved refugee problem plaguing Bangladesh without the Government of Myanmar taking appropriate action to assure repatriation with security and basic welfare. In light of its assessment, the mission recommends that the UNSC "ensure accountability for crimes under international law committed by Myanmar, preferably by referring the situation to the International Criminal Court or alternatively by creating an *ad hoc* international criminal tribunal".

On September 6, 2018, acting in Pre-Trial Chamber, the ICC issued its decision on the prosecutor's request for a ruling on ICC jurisdiction under Article 19(3) of the Rome Statute but also under Article 12(2)(a) "over the alleged deportation of the Rohingya people from Myanmar to Bangladesh" (ICC, 2018).[28] In issuing its decision, the judges accounted for the fact that the Government of Myanmar "declined to engage with the ICC by way of a formal reply".[29] The chamber judges observed that "as Bangladesh is a State Party to the [Rome] Statute, the body of 'applicable international laws' on the territory of Bangladesh comprises the Statute".[30] Despite the public pronouncements of the Government of Myanmar, "the Chamber observes that, under particular circumstances, the Statute may have an effect on States not Party to the Statute, consistent with principles of international law",[31] including here "quasi-universal treaties", "Additional Protocols", "customary law" (recognizing here "a 'progressive evolution' of custom"), and "well-established interpretations of the laws of war". Recognizing the limited scope of its proceedings at the time of decision, the chamber distinguished between the question of *law* (i.e., concerning its jurisdiction) and the question of *fact* (i.e., findings of fact concerning the alleged "deportation" and/or "forcible transfer" of population), allowing that these two actions are "among the crimes against humanity within the jurisdiction *ratione materiae* of the Court".[32] Following pertinent argument, the chamber concluded that "acts of deportation initiated in a State not Party to the Statute (through expulsion or other coercive acts) and completed in a State Party to the Statute (by virtue of victims crossing the border to a State) fall within the parameters of article 12(2)(a) of the Statute", and hence, "the Court has jurisdiction over the alleged deportation of members of the Rohingya people from Myanmar to Bangladesh".[33]

Response by the Government of Myanmar

On August 9, 2018, the Government of Myanmar issued a press release from the Ministry of the Office of the State Counsellor rejecting action such as recommended by the mission (Government. . ., 2018). This is consistent with an earlier statement from the Government of Myanmar issued on April 13, 2018. In the statement of August 9, 2018, the government reminded first of all that "Myanmar is not party to the Rome Statute", in which case "the Court [the ICC] has no jurisdiction on Myanmar whatsoever", and the government "categorically rejects the proposition that the Court has jurisdiction". On that basis, the government objected to the ICC prosecutor's request "for a Ruling on Jurisdiction under Article 19(3) of the Statute" as a "bad faith (*mala fides*)" action.

The government insisted on respect for its national sovereignty and territorial integrity, which "would permit it to continue to investigate all violations of international humanitarian law whether committed by its own forces or by elements hostile to the Government authorities such as the forces of the Arakan Rohingya Salvation Army ('ARSA')". Appealing implicitly to the principle of complementarity, the ministry reminded that it established an Independent Commission of Enquiry on July 30, 2018, charged to investigate allegations of human rights violations. The ministry noted that the ICC prosecutor was partial in the evidence assessed and not transparent, including "when Bangladesh chose to file its observations with the Court confidentially". Myanmar thereby had inadequate opportunity for formal response, were the government to do so.

Relative to claims of atrocity, the ministry objected to "mostly charged narratives of harrowing personal tragedies" that are not proper "legal issues", in which case such narratives are "prejudicial" and by no means "probative". Moreover, the fact of the refugee movement into Bangladesh, the ministry argued, although factually "across a boundary" legally, this did not amount to a "crime of deportation". Similarly, speaking at the UNSC session of August 28, 2018, the representative of Myanmar took note of the country's "democratic transition" and its desire for a peaceful, constructive, and caring resolution of the conflict at issue while being clear that the actions of ARSA (allegedly supported by "foreign terrorist organizations") were unacceptable for reasons of national security. The government representative noted Myanmar's commitment to bilateral agreements on "voluntary" repatriation of refugees (i.e., "verified displaced persons") made with the Government of Bangladesh. The representative of Myanmar addressed the issue of accountability following national law without any mandate for international jurisdiction. At issue here was the "objectivity, impartiality and sincerity" of the mission, hence objection to its findings of fact.[34] In contrast, the representative of Bangladesh accepted the findings of fact to support international jurisdiction: "[w]ith such conclusions at hand, the Security Council's custodianship of the issue remains all the more relevant and pressing", especially in view of the "culture of impunity for the alleged crimes".[35]

Following the ICC Chamber decision of September 6, 2018, the Government of Myanmar rejected the decision on grounds of "faulty procedure" and "dubious legal merit". Indeed, the government argued, "The over-extended application of jurisdiction challenges the fundamental principles of legal certainty and is contrary to accepted principles of public international law. It has created a dangerous precedent and erodes the moral authority of the Court" ("Myanmar Turns Down . . .", 2018).

Applicable principles of international justice

As is well-known among scholars of international law, after World War 2 the governments of the Allied Powers (the United States, the Provisional French Republic, the UK–Great Britain and Northern Ireland, and the USSR) took it upon themselves to constitute an International Military Tribunal by way of a joint charter agreement. They did so for the express purpose of bringing war criminals of the European Axis (Hitler's Nazi Germany and Mussolini's fascist Italy) before the bar of justice.[36] The signatory parties acted "in the interests of all the United Nations" even as the agreement did not prejudice the jurisdiction of national courts in Allied Territories for trial of those individuals charged with war crimes. What mattered was that such crimes not go unpunished.

The articles of the agreement stipulated the tribunal's jurisdiction and general principles. Article 6 identified several categories of crime that are well recognized today – crimes against peace originating in war of aggression, war crimes violating the laws or customs of war, and crimes against humanity. Those subject to the tribunal's jurisdiction included leaders, organizers, instigators, and accomplices "participating in the formulation or execution of a common plan or conspiracy to commit any of the foregoing crimes". Article 7 is explicitly clear that neither official position nor following superior orders frees a defendant from personal responsibility. The reference to the laws or customs of war presupposes the Hague Conventions of October 18, 1907.

It was not surprising, then, that in 1950 the UN International Law Commission adopted the principles of international law recognized in the Charter of the Nuremberg Tribunal and in the judgment rendered by the tribunal.[37] These principles remain pertinent in their declaration of duty: any *person* committing a crime *under international law* being responsible and liable to punishment. The presupposition here is that international law "may impose duties on individuals directly without any interposition of internal [i.e., national/domestic] law". Furthermore, Principle II stipulates that "[t]he fact that internal law does not impose a penalty for an act which constitutes a crime under international law does not relieve the person who committed the act from responsibility under international law". This principle presupposes the "supremacy" of international law over national law, such that "international law can bind individuals even if national law does not direct them to observe the rules of international law". As stated in the Charter of the Nuremberg Tribunal, "the very essence of the Charter is that individuals have international duties which transcend national obligations of obedience imposed by the individual state". Of course, Principle V is also clear that *culpability* under international law assumes, but also expects it to be demonstrated, that a "moral choice" was in fact possible for an individual alleged to have committed a crime. Specifically, the commission reminded of the tribunal's rationale, holding that the law of nations (*jus gentium*) does not recognize (and has never recognized) as a legitimate defense the fact that a soldier was ordered to kill or torture or otherwise commit "acts of brutality" in violation of the international law of war.

Granted, UN member states committed in December 1965 to the Declaration on the Inadmissibility of Intervention in the Domestic Affairs of the States and the Protection of Their Independence and Sovereignty.[38] The declaration considers not only armed intervention contrary to the principle of self-determination but also that "all forms of indirect intervention are contrary" to this principle, especially relative to self-determination after a nation has freed itself from colonialism. The declaration prohibits intervention and interference in the "civil strife" of a given state. That said, however, the declaration prohibits the use of force "to deprive peoples of their national identity" insofar as this "constitutes a violation of their inalienable rights". This prohibition is applicable not merely to a foreign power but also to a state having civil strife; for rights that are inalienable in the sense intended here are "human rights" and "fundamental freedoms", not merely civil rights otherwise protected by national law (which is why the final statement of the declaration appeals to the authority of the UN Charter).

Given the importance of human rights and fundamental freedoms, in November 1968 states parties agreed there is no statute of limitations to war crimes and crimes against humanity.[39] The Convention notes that "the application to war crimes and crimes against humanity of the rules of municipal law relating to the period of limitation for ordinary crimes is a matter of serious concern to world public opinion, since it prevents the prosecution and punishment of persons responsible for those crimes". In that case "it is necessary and timely to affirm in international law . . . the principle that there is no period of limitation for war crimes and crimes against humanity, and *to secure its universal application*".[40] This latter provision *does not presume state consent when municipal law is inadequate relative to the protection of human rights and fundamental freedoms*. Further, Article II of the Convention thereby holds accountable both

> representatives of State authority and private individuals who, as principals or accomplices, participate in or who directly incite others to the commission of any of those crimes, or who conspire to commit them, irrespective of the degree of completion, and to representatives of the State authority who tolerate their commission.

The terms of this article remain in force whether a state is a consenting party or not.

This Convention was followed, in December 1973, by international commitment to principles of international cooperation in the detection, arrest, extradition, and punishment of persons guilty of war crimes and crimes against humanity.[41] It is amply clear that, therefore, as a matter of both moral and legal principle, "[w]ar crimes and crimes against humanity, wherever they are committed, shall be subject to investigation and the persons whom there is evidence that they have committed such crimes shall be subject to tracing, arrest, trial and, if found guilty, to punishment". Granted, recognizing the principle of sovereignty and the principle of complementarity, it is conceded that "[e]very State has the right to try its own nationals for war crimes against humanity" and is expected to "take the domestic and international measures necessary" without appeal to "legislative or other measures which may be prejudicial to the international obligations" assumed.

There is no doubt, therefore, that the Government of Myanmar is morally and legally *obligated* by the foregoing general principles of international law and justice. Further, inasmuch as the armed conflict is initially domestic, despite the cross-border refugee problem, Myanmar has a *responsibility to protect* civilians when they are victims of non-international armed conflict, including armed conflict between a state's "armed forces and dissident armed forces or other organized armed groups".[42] This protocol stipulates a "Personal Field of Application" (Article 2) such that the terms are to be applied "without any adverse distinction founded on race, colour, sex, language, religion or belief, political or other opinion, national or social origin, wealth, birth or other status . . . to all persons affected by an armed conflict". This protocol applies to the current conflict in Myanmar's Rakhine state even as it is recognized (Article 3) that the Government of Myanmar has the right "to maintain or re-establish law and order" in that part of its national territory and otherwise "to defend the national unity and territorial integrity of the State". Article 4 stipulates further that non-belligerent parties (hence, including here Rohingya civilians as "Myanmar nationals") are "entitled to respect for their person, honour and convictions and religious practices".

Undoubtedly this applies to all members of the Muslim community of Rakhine state, who shall not suffer discrimination merely because they are Muslim, and who, as a "civilian population" and as "individual civilians", "shall enjoy general protection against the dangers arising from military operations". This is certainly to be understood essential in the case of the Government of Myanmar's military operations, its so-called clearance operations, undertaken against the militant Muslim group ARSA. In this regard, Myanmar is accountable to *uphold* fundamental rules of international humanitarian law applicable in armed conflicts even as it is obligated to *eliminate* "all forms of intolerance and of discrimination based on religion and belief".[43] Similarly, the Government of Myanmar has an obligation to protect the rights of persons who are ethnic, religious, and linguistic minorities, such as the Rohingya. This is a general obligation stipulated by UN General Resolution on December 18, 1992.[44]

Conclusion

The French existentialist philosopher Albert Camus's reflections on "the human crisis" affecting France, Europe, and the world in the early years after World War 2 remain pertinent today. Camus (1946) observed that "there's a generation who thinks that anyone who places his hopes in the human condition is mad, but that anyone who despairs of events is a coward. This generation", Camus opined, "refuses absolute explanations and the rule of political philosophies, but wishes to affirm men and women in their flesh and their striving for liberty. . . . Because the world is absurd, we must provide it with all its meaning". And so, societies issue forth their declarations of meaning, especially through all the historical narratives that give their life-world meaning within the politics of identity diversely manifest in the modern nation-state system. Within this structure of international institutions and behavior, the fact is that policy, law, and morality are inextricably related. They are related all the more starkly, yet ambiguously, when engaging in war crimes and crimes against humanity. In the case of genocide, even if and when both policy and law fall short of considerations of proportionate retributive justice, the demand for moral accountability remains. Genocide always falls outside the categories of conventional criminality, not in the sense that someone declares such atrocities a monstrosity but certainly in the sense that genocide presents us with *radical evil* we shall not ignore.

Philosophers such as Hannah Arendt and Jacques Derrida, who have discussed such evil, leave us wondering whether there can ever be any "proportionate punishment" for such crimes. One is compelled to judge this category of criminality altogether unforgivable with punishment therefore in some sense both "inadequate and absurd" (Perrone-Moisés, 2006). Thus, Arendt (1973) asked, "What meaning has the concept of murder, when we are confronted with the mass production of corpses?" Indeed, "[t]his kind of criminality seems to transcend all moral categories and explode all standards of jurisdiction" (Arendt, 2003). Such insights, although delivered with reference to the unprecedented Nazi genocide of European Jews, nonetheless have their meaning for all subsequent genocides. This includes the combination of war crimes, crimes against humanity, and genocide ostensibly committed against the Rohingya. In due course, the ICC may proceed with reasonable authority and established jurisdiction over these crimes, or failing that, the International Court of Justice may be petitioned at the least to issue an advisory opinion that has moral probity.

Philosophically, one may decry the lack of proportionate retributive justice for the historically evident persecution of the Rohingya within Myanmar. Myanmar's Buddhist "communitarian" *ethos* has long championed the view that Buddhists in Rakhine state "protected the 'Western Gate' of the country and held fast against demographic pressure from Muslim Bengal" (International Crisis Group, 2017), thus to help preserve Buddhism in postcolonial Burma. This is a claim having its nationalist and religio-centric, thus ideological, appeal. But that view is today challenged – with justification of preponderant evidence – by the Rohingya refugee crisis and the "universalist" *ethos* that privileges human rights as a condition *sine qua non* of any contemporary national-state's political culture, whatever the claims to territorial sovereignty. And herein lays the moral-philosophical dilemma, without resolution there can be no efficacious policy that resolves the crisis. The international community cannot fail to contest this criminality, lest the impunity of radical evil declare itself the victor against the extant *jus gentium*.

The "scandal of the refugee" from Myanmar occurs in the presence of disputed historical narratives, wherein history is all too often a "history of errors" or assumed to be a matter of insuperable and inalterable "fate", as Camus (1946) observed. It therefore behooves all parties concerned to insist on justice and liberty, on both *human* rights (not mere civil rights) and *fundamental freedoms*, thus to affirm the rights and freedoms of the men, women, and children of the Rohingya – *no matter* the "imaginary geography" that holds people captive to the logic of statecraft with its antiquated principle of sovereignty. Despite the absurdities and seeming futility present in the scandal of the refugee, one must choose (as Camus counseled) to be neither executioner nor victim. Thereby one acts to forestall the single act of murder that leads all too inexorably to genocide.

Notes

1 Although Bangladesh is at the forefront of the recent exodus, the fact is that multiple countries over recent time have received dislocated Rohingya – India, Pakistan, Malaysia, Thailand, Nepal, Indonesia, Saudi Arabia, and the United States.
2 UNHCR, *Convention and Protocol Relating to the Status of Refugees*, p. 15.
3 The concept of imaginary geography has been used by international law scholar Richard A. Falk in venues of public lecture and in his writings involving world order studies and the challenges involving transformation of international institutional structures and patterns of behavior as well as transformation of philosophical orientation or values. In this regard, see Swazo, 2002. See also, more generally, Marshall, 2015; more specifically, see Chapman, 2009.
4 See here World Health Organization Weekly Situation Report #32, 2018, See more recently Bi-weekly Situation Report #04, February 28, 2019.
5 United Nations, General Assembly, 2018; see document A/C.3/73/L.51.
6 With Myanmar and Bangladesh both contracting parties to the Genocide Convention, it is clear Myanmar is obligated under Article I to prevent and punish the crime of genocide *as a crime of international law*, not as a domestic crime. If it does not, Bangladesh is within its rights, under Article IX, to submit the matter to the International Court of Justice for an advisory opinion.
7 See also Gerver, "Would It Be Ethical for the UN Refugee Agency to Send Rohingya Back to Myanmar?" 2018. Gerver writes, in the latter article, "UNHCR faces an ethical dilemma that my research has identified and attempted to resolve. I call it the Consent Dilemma: On the one hand, if UNHCR helps refugees repatriate, many will return who have no reasonable alternative, and so perhaps their choices are involuntary. If UNHCR has failed to obtain refugees' voluntary consent, it may be acting unethically in helping them return. On the other hand, if UNHCR is fairly certain refugees will remain detained and destitute in Bangladesh, helping with return may seem the best option".
8 Parenthetical remarks are those of Yanghee Lee, UN special rapporteur for Myanmar, as cited by Ellis-Petersen, 2018.
9 Also see Dillabough-Lefebvre, 2018a. The latter reports on the presentation of Bangladesh Foreign Secretary Md. Shahidul Haque "Rohingya Humanitarian Crisis: Bangladesh's Response" at the LSE South Asia Centre on March 15, 2018. See also Dillabough-Lefebvre, 2018b.
10 For a summary, see Brunnstrom, 2018.
11 European Parliament, RC-B8–0371–2018, adopted September 13, 2019 as P8_TA-PROV(2018)0345.
12 See here Burma Citizenship Law (Pyithu Hluttaw Law No. 4 of 1982), 2018. This act/law specifies (II.3) that nationals of ethnic groups "that have settled in any of the territories included within the State as their permanent home from a period prior to 1185B.E., 1823 A.D., are Burma citizens". Nonetheless, II.8(a) stipulates when "in the interest of the State, the Council of State may confer on any person citizenship or associate citizenship or naturalized citizenship" consistent with the definitions given.
13 Rütland here refers to Leider, 2013.
14 The Constitution of the Union of Burma, September 24, 1947, effective January 4, 1948, 2018.
15 Leider here cites Selth, 2003, 14–15.

16 Leider refers to Chris Lewa's "authoritative paper" presented at the Canadian Friends of Burma Public Conference in 2002, titled "The Refugee Situation on the Western Borders of Burma", which argues that "the Rohingya Muslims are ethnically and religiously related to the Chittagongians of southern Bangladesh".
17 Leider cites an American Baptist missionary writing in the early 1800s (from 1834 to 1844) that "many Bengalee Mussulmans" immigrated to Arakan, "to get higher wages and better living, than they could procure in Chittagong".
18 The State Department seems to have committed minimally to a charge of ethnic cleansing.
19 The Pre-Trial Chamber of the ICC has authorized the Office of the Prosecutor to proceed with a preliminary examination for the purpose of investigating claims of the crime of deportation, which may or may not lead to further investigation for crimes subject to ICC jurisdiction in the absence of the Government of Myanmar initiating investigation and prosecution.
20 See also van Schaack, 2018b, 201. For a prior discussion see Ibrahim, 2016.
21 See here Ahmed, 2018.
22 United Nations Security Council, S/PV.8333, 8333rd Meeting, August 28, 2018, p. 2/29.
23 Human Rights Council, 39th Session. Detailed findings are given in document A/HRC/39/CRP.2.
24 A/HRC/39/64, p. 15.
25 A/HRC/39/64, p. 16.
26 A/HRC/39/64, p. 17.
27 A/HRC/39/64, p. 18.
28 International Criminal Court, 2018. The prosecutor's request was filed on April 9, 2018.
29 ICC-RoC46(3)-01/18, p. 9/50.
30 ICC-RoC46(3)-01/18, p. 16/50.
31 ICC-RoC46(3)-01/18, p. 25/50.
32 ICC-RoC46(3)-01/18, p. 31/50.
33 ICC-RoC46(3)-01/18, p. 42/50.
34 UNSC, S/PV.833, p. 26/29.
35 UNSC, S/PV.833, pp. 26–27/29.
36 See here 82 U.N.T.S. 279, concluded at London and entered into force on August 8, 1845.
37 See here UN Doc. A/1316, *Yearbook of the International Law Commission* (2 Y.B.I.L.C. 374) (1950).
38 Adopted by the UN General Assembly, December 21, 1965, GA Res. 2131, UN GAOR, 20th Session, Supp. No. 14, at 11, UN Doc. A/6014 (1966).
39 Convention on the Non-Applicability of Statutory Limitations to War Crimes and Crimes Against Humanity. Adopted by the UN General Assembly, November 26, 1968, entered into force November 11, 1970, UNGA Res. 2391 (Annex), UN GAOR, 23rd Sess., Supp. No. 18, at 40, UN Doc. A/7218 (1969).
40 Convention on the Non-Applicability of Statutory Limitations to War Crimes and Crimes Against Humanity. Adopted by the UN General Assembly, November 26, 1968, entered into force November 11, 1970, UNGA Res. 2391 (Annex), UN GAOR, 23rd Sess., Supp. No. 18, at 40, UN Doc. A/7218 (1969), italics added.

41 Principles of International Co-operation in the Detection, Arrest, Extradition and Punishment of Persons Guilty of War Crimes and Crimes Against Humanity, adopted by the UN General Assembly, December 3, 1973, GA Res. 3074, 28th Sess. Supp. No. 30, at 78, UN Doc. A/9030 (1974).

42 Protocol Additional (No. II) to the Geneva Conventions of August 12, 1949, and Relating to the Protection of Victims of Non-International Armed Conflicts, concluded at Geneva, June 8, 1977, entered into force December 7, 1978. U.N.J.Y.B. 135; 1977 Misc. 19, Cmnd. 6927.

43 United Nations General Assembly Resolution on the Elimination of All Forms of Intolerance and of Discrimination Based on Religion and Belief, adopted November 23, 1981, GA Res. 36/55, UN GAOR, 36th Sess., Supp. No. 51, at 171, UN Doc. A/36/684 (1981).

44 Declaration of the Rights of Persons Belonging to National or Ethnic, Religious and Linguistic Minorities, adopted by the UN General Assembly, December 18, 1992, GA Res. 47/135 (Annex), UN GAOR, 47th Sess., Supp. No. 49, at 210, UN Doc. A/RES/47/135 (1992).

References

Ahmed, B., Orcutt, M., Sammonds, P., Burns, R., Issa, R., Abubakar, I., & Devakumar, D. (2018, May). Humanitarian disaster for Rohingya refugees: Impending natural hazards and worsening public health crises. *The Lancet Global Health*, *6*, e487–488. Retrieved October 13, 2018, from www.thelancet.com/action/showPdf?pii=S2214-109X%2818%2930125-6

Ahmed, F. U. (2018, May 30). Bangladesh's observations on Rohingya deportation. *The Daily Star*. Retrieved October 15, 2018, from www.thedailystar.net/opinion/human-rights/bangladesh-observations-rohingya-deportation-1583471

AlTamimi, Y. (2018). Human rights and the excess of identity: A legal and theoretical inquiry into the notion of identity in Strasbourg case law. *Social & Legal Studies*, *27*(3), 283–298. Retrieved November 7, 2018, from http://journals.sagepub.com/doi/full/10.1177/0964663917722598.

Arendt, H. (1973). *The origins of totalitarianism*. New York: Harvest Book.

Arendt, H. (2003). *Personal responsibility under dictatorship*. New York: Shocken Books.

"Bangladesh Seals Off Border with Myanmar Amid Fresh Influx of Refugees". (2019, February 7). *The Times of India*. Retrieved February 17, 2019, from https://timesofindia.indiatimes.com/world/south-asia/bangladesh-seals-off-border-with-myanmar-amid-fresh-influx-of-refugees/articleshow/67885243.cms.

Berkley Forum, Berkley Center for Religion, Peace & World Affairs. (2017, October 24). *Religion and the persecution of Rohingya Muslims*. Retrieved November 1, 2018, from https://berkleycenter.georgetown.edu/posts/religion-and-the-persecution-of-rohingya-muslims

Bi-weekly Situation Report #04. (2019, February 28). Retrieved March 12, 2019, from www.searo.who.int/bangladesh/bi-weeklysitrep04cxbban2019.pdf

Brassard, F. (2006). The path of the bodhisattva and the creation of oppressive cultures. In M. Zimmerman (Ed.), *Buddhism and violence* (pp. 11–24). Lumbini: Lumbini International Research Institute.

Brunnstrom, D. (2018, December 3). Human rights law group calls for tribunal on crimes against Rohingya. *Reuters News*. Retrieved December 5, 2018, from www.reuters.com/article/us-usa-myanmar-rohingya/human-rights-law-group-calls-for-tribunal-on-crimes-against-rohingya-idUSKBN1O21K8?feedType=RSS&feedName=topNews

Burma Citizenship Law (Pyithu Hluttaw Law No. 4 of 1982). Retrieved October 8, 2018, from http://eudo-citizenship.eu/NationalDB/docs/1982%20Myanmar%20Citizenship%20Law%20%5BENGLISH%5D.pdf

Camus, A. (1946, March 28). *The human crisis*. Retrieved April 4, 2020, from www.reddit.com/r/philosophy/comments/4uz1tc/transcript_of_albert_camus_the_human_crisis/

Chang, C., Yasin, D., Dwip, S. P., Kenyon, D., & Lederer, E. M. (2017, September 17). *Violence in Myanmar shows the world needs to stop romanticizing Buddhism*. Retrieved November 1, 2018, from www.news.com.au/world/asia/violence-in-myanmar-shows-the-world-needs-to-stop-romanticising-buddhism/news-story/37bf65e55ec59eb1922f82942576161a

Chapman, G. P. (2009). *The geopolitics of South Asia* (3rd ed.). Burlington, VT: Ashgate Publishing.

Chen, A. (2018, October 5). A philosopher explains how our addiction to stories keeps Us from understanding history: How history gets things wrong. *The Verge*. Retrieved October 8, 2018, from www.theverge.com/2018/10/5/17940650/how-history-gets-things-wrong-alex-rosenberg-interview-neuroscience-stories

The Constitution of the Union of Burma, 24 September 1947, effective 04 January 1948. Retrieved November 8, 2018, from www.ilo.org/dyn/natlex/docs/ELECTRONIC/79573/85699/F1436085708/MMR79573.pdf

"Decision on the Admissibility of the Case Pursuant to Article 19(2)(b) of the Statute". (2011, August 20). *Ruto, Kosgey and Sang* (ICC-01/09–011/11 OA), Appeals Chamber.

Dillabough-Lefebvre, D. (2018a). *Bangladesh's response to one of the biggest refugee crises of the century (Part 1)*. LSE South Asia Centre. Retrieved October 15, 2018, from http://blogs.lse.ac.uk/southasia/2018/04/19/bangladeshs-response-to-one-of-the-biggest-refugee-crisis-of-the-century-part-1/

Dillabough-Lefebvre, D. (2018b). *Repatriation, refoulement and Rohingya nationality: Bangladesh's response to one of the biggest refugee crises of the century (Part 2)*. LSE South Asia Centre. Retrieved October 15, 2018, from http://blogs.lse.ac.uk/southasia/2018/05/02/repatriation-refoulement-and-rohingya-nationality-bangladeshs-response-to-one-of-the-biggest-refugee-crises-of-the-century-part-2/

Dillon, M. (1998, December). The scandal of the refugee: Some reflections on the 'inter' of international relations. *Refuge*, *17*(6), 30–39.

Ellis-Petersen, H. (2018, November 21). What next for the Rohingya? *The Guardian*. Retrieved November 22, 2018, from www.theguardian.com/world/2018/nov/22/what-next-for-the-rohingya

European Parliament. Resolution of 19 September 2019 on Myanmar, P9_TA (2019) 0018, https://www.europa.eu/docco/document/TA-2019-0018_EN.html.

Gerver, M. (2018a). *The ethics and practice of refugee repatriation*. Edinburgh: Edinburgh University Press.

Gerver, M. (2018b, December 17). Would it be ethical for the U.N. refugee agency to send Rohingya back to Myanmar? *Washington Post*. Retrieved December 19, 2018, from www.washingtonpost.com/news/monkey-cage/wp/2018/12/17/would-it-be-ethical-for-the-u-n-refugee-agency-to-send-rohingyas-back-to-myanmar/?noredirect=on&utm_term=.16a641c1f071

Government of Myanmar. (2018, October 24). *Statement by Ambassador Hau Do Suan, permanent representative of the republic of the union of Myanmar to the United Nations at Security Council briefing by HRC-FFM*. Retrieved November 13, 2018, from http://myanmarmissionnewyork.org/images/pdf/2018/Statements/Final%20and%20as%20delivered%20Myanmar%20PR%20statement%20at%20SC%20Open%20briefing%20on%2024%20Oct.pdf

Haviland, C. (2015, May 30). The darker side of Buddhism. *BBC News Magazine*. Retrieved November 1, 2018, from www.bbc.com/news/magazine-32929855

Human Rights Council, 39th Session, 10–28 September 2018, Agenda Item No. 4, *Report of the independent international fact-finding mission on Myanmar*, A/HRC/39/64.

Ibrahim, A. (2016). *The Rohingyas: Inside Myanmar's hidden genocide*. London: C. Hurst & Co.

International Center for Diarrheal Disease Research, Bangladesh. (2018, April 25). *Rohingya population displacement: Concern for spread of drug-resistant Malaria?* Retrieved November 7, 2018, from www.icddrb.org/component/news/?id=841&task=view

International Criminal Court, Pre-Trial Chamber 1. (2018, September 6, April 9). Decision on the 'prosecution's request for a ruling on jurisdiction under article 19(3) of the Statute, ICC-RoC46(3)-01/18. The Prosecutor's request was filed.

International Crisis Group. (2017, September 5). Buddhism and state power in Myanmar. *Crisis Group Asia Report No. 290*. Brussels, Belgium.

Jerryson, M. (2015). Buddhists and violence: Historical continuity/academic incongruities. *Religion Compass*, *9*(5), 141–150. Retrieved November 1, 2018, from https://onlinelibrary.wiley.com/doi/pdf/10.1111/rec3.12152

Jerryson, M. (2017, October 13). *Buddhist inspired genocide*. Berkley Forum, Berkley Center for Religion, Peace & World Affairs. Retrieved November 1, 2018, from https://berkleycenter.georgetown.edu/responses/buddhist-inspired-genocide

Keyes, C. (2016). Theravada Buddhism and Buddhist nationalism: Sri Lanka, Myanmar, Cambodia, and Thailand. *The Review of Faith and International Affairs*, *14*(4), 42–52.

Kleine, C. (2006). Evil monks with good intentions? Remarks on Buddhist monastic violence and its doctrinal background. In M. Zimmerman (Ed.), *Buddhism and violence* (pp. 65–98). Lumbini: Lumbini International Research Institute.

Leider, J. P. (2013). Rohingya: The name, the movement and the quest for identity. In *Nation building in Myanmar* (pp. 204–255, 234–235, 241). Yangon: Myanmar EGRESS/Myanmar Peace Centre. Retrieved October 7, 2018, from https://s3.amazonaws.com/academia.edu.documents/34461018/LEIDER_Rohingya_Name_Movement__Identity_14_06.pdf?AWSAccessKeyId=AKIAIWOWYYGZ2Y53UL3A&Expires=1538878459&Signature=6CQ16DMKoRgcVc%2BxjtS%2F0ZEiwaQ%3D&response-content-disposition=inline%3B%20filename%3DRohingya_The_name_the_movement_the_ques.pdf

MacGregor, N. (2017, October 5). Belief is back: Why the world is putting its faith in religion. *The Guardian.* Retrieved October 8, 2018, from www.theguardian.com/books/2018/oct/05/belief-is-back-societies-worldwide-faith-religion

Marshall, K. (2017, October 23). *Religious factors in the Rohingya crisis: A horrific state of limbo.* Berkley Forum, Berkley Center for Religion, Peace & World Affairs. Retrieved November 1, 2018, from https://berkleycenter.georgetown.edu/responses/religious-factors-in-the-rohingya-crisis-a-horrific-state-of-limbo

Marshall, T. (2015). *Prisoners of geography.* London: Elliott and Thompson Limited.

McPherson, P., Lewis, S., Aung, T. T., Naing, S., & Siddiqui, Z. (2018, December 18). Special report: Myanmar's moves could mean the Rohingya never go home. *Reuters News.* Retrieved December 19, 2018, from www.reuters.com/article/us-myanmar-rohingya-return-special-repor/special-report-myanmars-moves-could-mean-the-rohingya-never-go-home-idUSKBN1OH1AK?feedType=RSS&feedName=topNews

Mumford, T. (2017, October 19). *Rohingya Muslims may the ultimate price for their religious and ethnic identity.* Berkley Forum, Berkley Center for Religion, Peace & World Affairs. Retrieved November 1, 2018, from https://berkleycenter.georgetown.edu/responses/rohingya-muslims-pay-the-ultimate-price-for-their-religious-and-ethnic-identity

Myanmar Ministry of Information. (2008). *Constitution of the republic of the union of Myanmar, 2008.* Retrieved November 8, 2018, from www.wipo.int/edocs/lexdocs/laws/en/mm/mm009en.pdf

"Myanmar Turns Down ICC's Majority Decision of the Pre-Trial Chamber 1". (2018, September 8). *The Nation.* Retrieved October 9, 2018, from www.nationmultimedia.com/detail/asean-plus/30354032

Noor, M., Thudi, M., Islam, S., & Forid, S. (2017). Rohingya crisis and the concerns for Bangladesh. *International Journal of Scientific & Engineering Research, 8*(12), 1192–1196.

OIC Okays Legal Action Against Myanmar. (2019, March 5). *The Daily Star.* Retrieved March 12, 2019, from www.thedailystar.net/southeast-asia/news/oic-okays-legal-action-against-myanmar-1710487

Papazoglou, A. (2019, January 15). The philosophical roots of today's immigration debate. *The New Republic.* Retrieved January 27, 2019, from https://newrepublic.com/article/152883/philosophical-roots-todays-immigration-debate

Perrone-Moisés, C. (2006, September). Forgiveness and crimes against humanity. *Zeitschrifte für Politisches Denken, Ausgabe, 1*(2). Retrieved November 3, 2018, from www.hannaharendt.net/index.php/han/article/view/90/146

Pillamarri, A. (2017, October 29). Buddhism and Islam in Asia: A long and complicated history. *The Diplomat.* Retrieved November 1, 2018, from https://thediplomat.com/2017/10/buddhism-and-islam-in-asia-a-long-and-complicated-history/

President's Office, The Republic of the Union of Myanmar. (2018). *Myanmar permanent representative made a statement on the UN security council's visit to Myanmar.* Retrieved November 13, 2018, from www.president-office.gov.mm/en/?q=issues/rakhine-state-affairs/id-8766

Public International Law & Policy Group. (2018, December). *Documenting atrocity crimes committed against the Rohingya in Myanmar's Rakhine state: Factual findings and legal analysis report*, IPLPG 2018 Human Rights Documentation Mission. Retrieved December 5, 2018, from https://static1.squarespace.com/static/5900b58e1b631bffa367167e/t/5c058268c2241b5f71a0535e/1543864941782/PILPG+-+ROHINGYA+REPORT+-+Factual+Findings+and+Legal+Analysis+-+3+Dec+2018+%281%29.pdf

"Rohingya Refugees: Aid Agencies seek $920M for This Year". (2019, February 16). *The Daily Star*. Retrieved February 17, 2019, from www.thedailystar.net/rohingya-crisis/news/un-seek-920m-rohingya-refugee-1702576

Rosenberg, A. (2018). *How history gets things wrong: The neuroscience of our addiction to stories*. Cambridge: MIT Press.

Rütland, A. (2017, May). *Myanmar's Rohingya problem in context*, ISPSW Strategy Series: Focus on Defense and International Security, Issue No. 485. Rütland here refers to Leider, 2013.

Selth, A. (2003). *Burma's Muslims" terrorists or terrorized?* (pp. 14–15). Canberra: Australian National University, Strategic and Defence Studies Centre.

Sumon, S. (2018, December 6). Rohingya refugees wary after Myanmar minister's hostile remarks. *Arab News*. Retrieved December 9, 2018, from www.arabnews.com/node/1416716/world.

Swazo, N. K. (2002). *Crisis theory and world order: Heideggerian reflections*. Albany: SUNY Press.

Swazo, N. K. (2007). *'Forgotten' humanitarian obligations: The case of the Saharawi*, African Studies Monographs, Serial No. VIII. Lagos Nigeria: Onosomegbowho Ogbinaka Publishers, Ltd., in collaboration with Society of Research on African Cultures, USA.

"Thousands Flee Clashes Between Buddhist Group and Myanmar Army". (2019, January 3). *Aljazeera News*. Retrieved February 17, 2019, from www.aljazeera.com/news/2019/01/thousands-flee-clashes-buddhist-group-myanmar-army-190102234329174.html.

UNESCO, International Bioethics Committee. (2017, September 15). *Report of the IBC on the bioethical response to the situation of refugees*, SHS/YES/IBC-24/17/2 REV.2, Paris. See here

United Nations, General Assembly. (2018, November 16). *Third committee, 73rd Session, 50th and 51st Meetings, GA/SHS/4254*. Retrieved November 22, 2018, from www.un.org/press/en/2018/gashc4254.doc.htm, Document A/C.3/73/L.51

United Nations High Commissioner for Refugees (UNHCR). (2010). *Convention and protocol relating to the status of refugees*. Geneva: UNHCR. Retrieved February 25, 2019, from www.unhcr.org/protection/basic/3b66c2aa10/convention-protocol-relating-status-refugees.html

United Nations Security Council (UNSC). (2018, February 13). S/PV-8179, 8179th Meeting, Tuesday.

United Nations Security Council (UNSC). (2018, August 28). S/PV.8333, 8333rd Meeting.

U.S. Department of State. (2018, August). *Documentation of atrocities in Northern Rakhine state*. Retrieved October 13, 2018, from www.state.gov/j/drl/rls/286063.htm

van Schaack, B. (2018a, September 28). Determining the commission of genocide in Myanmar: Legal and policy considerations. *Social Science Research Network*. Retrieved October 13, 2018, from https://papers.ssrn.com/sol3/papers.cfm?abstract_id=3256591

van Schaack, B. (2018b, October 1). *Why what's happening to the Rohingya is genocide, just security organization*. Retrieved October 13, 2018, from www.justsecurity.org/60912/happening-rohingya-genocide/

Wade, F. (2017, September 15). Buddhists in Myanmar are unifying behind a deadly nationalism. *The Nation*. Retrieved November 1, 2018, from www.thenation.com/article/buddhists-in-myanmar-are-unifying-behind-a-deadly-nationalism/

Westcott, B., & George, S. (2017, September 13). Buddha would have helped persecuted Rohingya refugees, Dalai Lama says. *CNN News*. Retrieved November 1, 2018, from https://edition.cnn.com/2017/09/11/asia/rohingya-dalai-lama-myanmar/index.html

Whitaker, J. (2017, September 13). *Revisiting the crisis in Burma and Buddhism's role in it*. Retrieved November 1, 2018, from https://buddhism-controversy-blog.com/2017/09/13/revisiting-the-crisis-in-burma-and-buddhisms-role-in-it/

World Health Organization. (2018). *Health humanitarian appeal for the Rohingya crisis: 2018, regional office for South-East Asia, 2018*. Retrieved October 16, 2018, from www.who.int/emergencies/crises/bgd/bangladesh-humanitarian-appeal-rohingya-crisis-2018.pdf?ua=1

World Health Organization Weekly Situation Report #32, 28 June 2018, for the period. (2018, June 20–26). Retrieved November 7, 2018, from www.searo.who.int/bangladesh/weeklysitrep32cxbban.pdf?ua=1

Wright, R., & Rivers, M. (2018). *Return to Rakhine: "Genocide never happened in this country"*. Retrieved October 20, 2018, from https://edition.cnn.com/2018/10/17/asia/inside-rakhine-state-intl/index.html

XChange Foundation. (2018, August 28). *'The Rohingya amongst Us': Bangladeshi perspectives on the Rohingya crisis*. Retrieved October 15, 2018, from http://xchange.org/bangladeshi-perspectives-on-the-rohingya-crisis-survey/

2 The Rohingya crisis and geopolitics
A public policy conundrum

Sk. Tawfique M. Haque and Tasmia Nower

Bangladesh, the largest destination for Rohingya refugees, has received large numbers of Rohingyas since 1978 in four phases – before the 1990s, after the 1990s, post-2012, and post-2017. In the aftermath of the post-2017 Rohingya crisis, the Government of Bangladesh permitted an additional 700,000 Rohingyas to take shelter in Bangladesh until their safe return to Myanmar. Bangladesh is now in a critical juncture of addressing the humanitarian needs of more than 1 million Rohingya refugees and their sustainable future repatriation. In the wake of the continuous influx of such large numbers of Rohingyas, the Government of Bangladesh has long been pursuing Myanmar, regional powers, and international communities for a long-lasting solution of the crisis. Despite the presence of all the evidence of ethnic conflict, the Rohingya crisis is no longer limited to an internal issue of a nation-state. The geopolitical dimensions of the recent conflict have made a greater impact on possible sustainable solutions of this crisis. The objective of this chapter is to analyze how and why the geopolitical dimensions have superseded the humanitarian aspects of the Rohingya crisis. This study focuses on the role of regional powers, for example, China and India, and also the regional blocs like Association of Southeast Asian Nations (ASEAN) in addressing this crisis. This study is based predominantly on document analysis and interviews. The nature of this research demanded some conceptual discussion on geopolitics. In the second phase, this chapter will explore the role of major powers of this region vis-à-vis the political and policy responses of the Government of Bangladesh to achieve a long–term, permanent solution of this age-old crisis.

Geopolitical strategies and the Rohingya crisis

Geopolitics refers to the power relationships among politics or states and geography, demography, and economy with regard to the foreign policy of a country (Patten, 2013). The term "geopolitics" was coined in 1899 by the

Swedish political scientist Rudolf Kjellen, even though the idea of geopolitics existed long before that as states conquered or formed alliances to pursue gains. However, modern geopolitics gained momentum "when the first fully connected 'closed' international system of states emerged, in which any significant changes would unavoidably trigger 'zero-sum game' struggles between the great powers" and countries became concerned about the impact of the "geographical attributes of states and their relative spatial locations" in international politics (Berryman, 2012). Geopolitics became even more relevant with the rise of emerging nations and/or regional powers (Nolte, 2010). For example, Brazil, Russia, China, India, and South Africa (BRICS) gained popularity as "the future emerging economic powers" in the early 21st century, and their geopolitical alliances have further contributed to their power in contemporary times. Detlef Nolte, in his research paper "How to Compare Regional Powers: Analytical Concepts and Research Topics" (2010), writes,

> The research departments [Goldman Sachs] of the investment banks prognosticated that at the end of the third or the during the fourth decade of the twenty-first century China will have overtaken the US as the largest economy, and that India may follow suit in the second half of the century.

As predicted, what we are seeing today is the rise of China and India, primarily due to their growing economies as a result of both geographic and politic strategic alliances.

Current geopolitics is not predominantly centered on "the acquisition of territory" but is based on commerce and economy carried out by states, which "still constituted the basic building blocks of the international system" (Berryman, 2012). Accordingly, geopolitics can be explained in terms of political geography and realism. As John Berryman (2012) states, geopolitics can be explained in terms of "a mix of political geography and realist international theory, [which] focused on ways in which the exercise of international political power is shaped and limited by geographical, spatial and technological imperatives". In fact, Zhengyu Wu (2018) makes a similar argument that geopolitics is a branch of realism, specifically "a particular form of realism that is based on the influence of the natural environments defined by geography and technology". This is not only due to the work of realist experts, such as Henry Kissinger and Zbigniew Brzezinski, who have used geopolitics to "rationalize strategic analyses or justify policy recommendations", but also because "geopolitics as a particular body of thought shares with mainstream realist theories the same theoretical assumptions or 'biases" (Wu, 2018). As such, realism is a leading theory that can be used to explain the geopolitical interests and alliances of China and India with Myanmar, respectively. The China–Myanmar bilateral relationship and/or the India–Myanmar relationship can be explained based on the idea that minor powers aim to develop and foster relationships with other states or powers to elevate their regional as well as global status. In fact, the British geographer Sir Halford Mackinder, in his popular lecture "The Geographical Pivot of History", discussed one of his master ideas "that control of the world would be determined by which power or powers controlled Eurasia, be it Russia or Germany, or an alliance between the two, or China" (Berryman, 2012).

During the time of Mackinder's lecture, the pivot point was imperial Russia; however, currently, China and India, to a certain extent, have become the pivots with their strategic interests and foreign policies in the international setting. India's strategic partnership with Myanmar is due to its Look East Policy (LEP). The goal of LEP is to establish India's economic and strategic connection with Southeast Asia, and Myanmar is vital to that. Myanmar provides the only physical connection and economic integration between India and Southeast Asia (Ramya, 2018). LEP would also cultivate India's alliance with ASEAN members (Ramya, 2018). India is strengthening and furthering its economic reach to situate itself as a regional power and emerging country globally, which explains its political interest in Myanmar, that is, due to its geographical location on the map. As such, India has continued to remain passive with the Government of Myanmar's repression of the Rohingya refugees and lack of response with regard to their repatriation in Myanmar. As realism argues, given international anarchy, India is in a competition with other states to maximize its security by establishing its economic power, and Myanmar is key to that.

China, on the other hand, already has "unimpeded access to the world's oceans along with substantial human and natural resources", establishing itself as the new geopolitical "pivot" in Asia (Berryman, 2012). As Robert Kaplan (2010) discusses in his paper "The Geography of Chinese Power", "China's virtual reach extends from Central Asia, with all its mineral and hydrocarbon wealth, to the main shipping lanes of the Pacific Ocean", and adding to that, China's billion-dollar project, the Belt and Road Initiative (BRI), makes China "stand at the hub of geopolitics" (Kaplan, 2010). The BRI is considered to be "the 21st Century Maritime Silk Road", comprised of infrastructure development and investments all the way from East Asia to Europe (Chatzky & McBride, 2019). According to the Council of Foreign Relations (2019), the BRI "is one of the most ambitious infrastructure projects ever conceived" and is a take on the original Silk Road that connected Europe to Asia (Chatzky & McBride, 2019). BRI would include "a vast network of railways, energy pipelines, highways, and streamlined border crossings, both westward – through the mountainous former Soviet republics – and southward, to Pakistan, India, and the rest of Southeast Asia" and East Africa (Chatzky & McBride, 2019). As such, Myanmar is vital in the construction of the BRI as Myanmar provides an economic corridor – the China–Myanmar Economic Corridor (CMEC) – as well as a Special Economic Zone (Peng, 2018). In addition to the BRI, the strategic bilateral relationship with Myanmar will also allow China to have easy access to Myanmar's energy and natural resources (Bolesta, 2018). The BRI has both huge economic and geopolitical implications for China, and to ensure them, China has to maintain a good, stable relationship with all the countries through which the BRI will be routed. In this international anarchic system, China is trying to maximize its security and power through economic expansion and establish its presence in the global setting.

In this power play of asserting and shaping the international system, both India and China are strategic players in the Rohingya crisis due to their geopolitical strategies. The strategic partnerships between China and Myanmar and India and Myanmar utilize geopolitics to pursue the states' respective goals and interests on the regional and global stage, which eventually have compromised the humanitarian concerns of this crisis. This plays a significant role in the Rohingya crisis, but before further delving into the impacts of geopolitics, it is important to analyze the relationship of Myanmar with Bangladesh, India, China, and ASEAN.

Bangladesh–Myanmar bilateral relationship

Myanmar is a very country compared to Bangladesh with an area of 676,577 square kilometers, whereas the area of Bangladesh is about 147,570 square kilometers. Whereas Myanmar has a population of around 54 million, with a density of 82 persons per kilometer, Bangladesh has a population of 165 million with a density of 1,252 people per square kilometer (Rashid, 2019). Another difference is the population in terms of religion: 89% of Myanmar's population is Buddhist, and 88% of Bangladesh's population is Muslim (Rashid, 2019). Being neighboring countries, they share about 271 kilometers of border, both on land and along the Naaf river (Rashid, 2019).

With regard to the bilateral relationship, there were two contentious issues between Myanmar and Bangladesh. The first was regarding the demarcation of the sea boundary between the two countries, which was finally settled in March 2012 by the 1982 International Tribunal of the Law of Sea Convention (Rashid, 2019). The maritime border issues between the two countries were a result of two factors. The first was due to a strong prospect of accessible gas in the part of the disputed area of the ocean. Second, there was a demand for gas on both sides. In Bangladesh, there was a growing demand for natural gas, given the power shortages in the country, which resulted in major domestic political issues. In addition to individual countries, there was a worldwide demand for gas, which Myanmar wanted to tap into. Myanmar's goal was that through gas exportation, it would be able to bring in foreign reserves and develop relationships with countries such as China and India (Bissinger, 2010). Although the maritime boundary dispute between the two states was peacefully resolved, the second historical issue over the Rohingya Muslims was never resolved and continues to be an ongoing issue between the two states (Bissinger, 2010). The Rohingya refugees' exodus from Myanmar to Bangladesh has been happening since the 1970s, eventually becoming a defining element in the bilateral relationship between the two states to the extent of affecting their position in other disputes (Parnini, Othman, & Ghazali, 2013). As such, even now, the Rohingya crisis is the main source of tension in the relationship between Myanmar and Bangladesh.

Since late 1970s, the Myanmar state has been reluctant to take or resettle the Rohingya refugees back to Myanmar. Comparatively, the Rohingyas themselves are not willing to be repatriated in Myanmar due to their fear of persecution by the Government of Myanmar. In the 1990s, Myanmar and Bangladesh tried negotiating the repatriation of the Rohingya refugees in Myanmar. Several documents were signed during that time period, such as a Memorandum of Understanding (MOU) between Bangladesh and Myanmar in April 1992. The MOU identified the terms for a repatriation program with limited UN High Commissioner for Refugees (UNHCR) involvement. Then, again in May 1993, another MOU was signed between the UNHCR and Bangladesh identifying the protection of these refugees in Bangladesh as well as their voluntary repatriation in Myanmar. A third attempt for repatriation was carried out in November 1993, when UNHCR and Myanmar signed an MOU to ensure the UNHCR's access to the returning refugees, identity cards, and the Rohingya's freedom of movement (Parnini et al., 2013). In the wake of the continuous influx of such large numbers of Rohingyas, the Government of Bangladesh has long been pursuing Myanmar for a long-lasting solution to the crisis. The bilateral initiatives with Myanmar have not been effective in dealing with peaceful and sustainable repatriation, mostly because of the Government of Myanmar and economic and strategic interests of regional and global powers.

In 2009, both Myanmar and Bangladesh restarted their bilateral negotiations, and repatriating the Rohingya refugees was a priority. In 2011, during the Bangladeshi foreign minister's visit to Myanmar, the minister stated, "Bangladesh was no longer willing to give shelter to Rohingya refugees, despite international calls for Bangladesh to open its border to them" (Parnini et al., 2013). In response, Myanmar authorities wanted to review the list of refugees to determine their citizenship status. This proved to be futile and a smokescreen because the Rohingyas were never offered the same citizenship that Buddhists and other groups enjoyed in Myanmar, particularly since 1982, when "Burma's junta passed a law that identified 135 ethnicities entitled to citizenship. The Rohingyas were not among them" (Calamur, 2017; Parnini et al., 2013). At the beginning of Myanmar's independence, the separate identity of Rohingya was recognized by the then democratic government of Premier U Nu (1948–1962). The situation worsened after the military takeover in 1962, leaving the Rohingyas subject to humiliating restrictions and harsh treatment by the state. In Myanmar, the Rohingyas became stateless, and this was institutionalized by the 1982 Citizenship Law (Haque, 2015).

The tense relationship over the Rohingya refugee crisis highly affected other bilateral issues between Myanmar and Bangladesh, mainly infrastructure projects, such as the Asian Highway, the Bay of Bengal Initiative for Multi-Sectoral Technical and Economic Cooperation (BIMSTEC), and the BCIM (Bangladesh, China, India, Myanmar) Corridor, which is intended to run through Rakhine state (Parnini et al., 2013). The dispute and tense relationship between the two countries over the Rohingya crisis have affected formal bilateral trade (Parnini et al., 2013); however, informal trade is still continuing (Kallol, 2017). According to Asif Showkat Kallol from the *Dhaka Tribune*, a leading newspaper in Bangladesh, "Founder President of the Bangladesh-Myanmar Chamber of Commerce and Industry (BMCCI), KB Ahmed, told that the actual volume of trade between the two countries is higher than the official figure, as the majority of trade between Myanmar and Bangladesh is informal" (Kallol, 2017).

Myanmar: bridge between India and Southeast Asia

India and Myanmar have long historical and cultural linkages. Myanmar has thousands of Indians living in Myanmar as a result of Indian emigration to Myanmar during British rule in this region (Ethirajan, 2015; Trivedi, 2018). In fact, Myanmar's growing opportunities for agriculture and trade attracted Indians over the centuries (Trivedi, 2018). During British rule, migration was due to a need for cheap Indian labor as well as middle-class intellectuals for administrative and civil service (Trivedi, 2018). Although colonialism and commerce played pivotal roles in connecting the two countries, currently the relationship is based more on geopolitics, such as through India's LEP.

Similar to China, Myanmar also has a close relationship with India due to its geographical location. In fact, one might say Myanmar even has a great geostrategic location due to its coastal position in the Bay of Bengal "between two competitive rising powers in Asia, i.e. India and China, and forms a land-bridge between South and Southeast Asia" (Lee, 2014). Even though both India and Myanmar have cultural overlaps, historical ties, and share a porous border that allows free movement of ethnic tribes, they have had a fraught relationship due to "colonial and postcolonial politics" (Ramya, 2018). As Ramya (2018) writes, "India's support for the democratic movement within Myanmar following the takeover by the military regime in 1962" played a key role in straining the bilateral relationship between the two states. However, since the 1990s, the bilateral relationship began to improve with the Myanmar junta through diplomacy, economic, and military strategies (Lee, 2014; Ramya, 2018). Gradually, Myanmar became more prominent in India's policy toward Southeast Asian countries from political, security, economic, and strategic perspectives. As pointed out by Yhome K. "Whether it was the desire to engage the eastern Asian regions or, more particularly, strengthening relations with the CLMV countries (Cambodia, Laos, Myanmar and Vietnam), India's renewed focus on them coincided with the strengthening of its bilateral ties with Myanmar" (Yhome, 2009). Both states initiated "high-level political and military exchanges" as well as "institutionalized bilateral cooperation on counterinsurgency and drug smuggling" (Lee, 2014).

With regard to economic connections, India was keen to develop its LEP, which required a close tie with its neighbor, Myanmar. The goal of LEP was to support India in developing its economic and strategic connection with Southeast Asia, of which Myanmar provides the only physical connection and economic integration between India and Southeast Asia (Ramya, 2018). Additionally, India envisioned that trade between India's northeast region and Myanmar would increase the trade with other ASEAN countries with the goal to "undercut the lure of insurgency and alleviating the considerable drain on internal security resources" needed to support the impoverished northeast region in India (Lee, 2014).

Part of India's LEP agenda includes the multimillion-dollar Kaladan project in Myanmar. As reported by Pallab Bhattacharya in the *Daily Star*, "India is fairly well invested in infrastructure development and human resources" in Myanmar, including the ambitious US$484-million Kaladan Multi-Modal Transit Transport project in Rakhine state (Bhattacharya, 2018). It is a "multi-modal sea, river and road transport corridor for shipment of cargo from the eastern ports of India to Myanmar through Sittwe port as well as to north-eastern part of India via Myanmar" (Chaudhary, 2019). It is highly significant to both India and Myanmar because it provides Myanmar with massive economic opportunities, opening up sea routes and economic development (PIB, The Hindu, 2019). In a similar manner, it is crucial to India because it will create a 1,328-kilometer route from Calcutta to Sittwe with the aim to decrease "the need to transport good through the narrow Siliguri corridor, also known as Chicken's Neck" in India (PIB, The Hindu, 2019). In short, the project connects Sittwe Port in Myanmar to the Indian-Myanmar border. The goal of this project is to achieve massive investment and trade as well as open up alternate routes that would connect to India's northeast region (Chaudhary, 2019). The Kaladan project has huge implications for the Rohingya crisis due to its detrimental effects. Sittwe, in southwestern Myanmar, is the capital of Rakhine state, which is also home to the Rohingya Muslims; the Sittwe port is located at the mouth of the Kaladan river. In fact, Rakhine state has massive economic potential. As reported by Chan Mya Htwe in the *Myanmar Times*, "Rakhine State holds enormous economic potential because the state has oil, natural gas fields and maritime resources from the Bay of Bengal", and the Kaladan project introduces more economic opportunity (Htwe, 2017).

Myanmar's abundant natural gas reserves were also of huge interest to India, given that India's domestic demand for gas and oil was climbing at a rapid pace. Myanmar will give India cheaper and more secure access to gas reserves than the alternative, which is "routes from Central Asia that would need to travel through Iran, or Afghanistan and Pakistan" (Lee, 2014). Another reason why India wanted to strengthen its bilateral ties with Myanmar was to prevent Myanmar from becoming a close ally of China (Engh, 2016). Since 1962, after China defeated India, it has perceived "China's growing strategic relationships with its immediate neighbors with suspicion and considers the possibility of its hostile encirclement as a core security threat" (Lee, 2014). As such, to the Indian state, it has been imperative to keep Myanmar from China's sphere of influence.

Additionally, Myanmar also became interested in developing its bilateral ties with India in the mid-1990s. This was due to several reasons: trade and economic development, diplomatic support, and military support – all these as a result of the West isolating Myanmar and putting pressure on Myanmar due to the military regime's political oppression (Lee, 2014). Diplomatic support from India was seen as vital in international organizations because India was perceived to be the largest democratic country in the world, thus allowing Myanmar to claim "legitimacy" (Lee, 2014). As Myanmar became isolated from the West, Myanmar was able to import military supplies from India as well as send their soldiers to India for training in counterinsurgency and defensive strategies (Lee, 2014). Economic cooperation between the two states became essential as Myanmar faced embargos and sanctions from the West (Lee, 2014). Another reason for Myanmar's growing engagement with India was to reduce its growing dependency on China. Western sanctions and embargos also caused Myanmar to become economically reliant on China, which Myanmar wanted to reduce by bringing India into its fold. As written in *The Diploma* in 2018, India provided "Myanmar an opportunity to counteract its overreliance on China and enhance its development and security prospects" (Ramya, 2018).

China–Myanmar bilateral relationship

Myanmar always had strong interactions with China. It can be traced back thousands of years, given "their geographic proximity and historic factors" (Bolesta, 2018). According to Myanmar historians, the historical relationship began in 802 AD, when the Pyu delegation to Chang-an, the capital of the Tang dynasty in then Myanmar, made the first diplomatic contact with China (Than, 2003). Following that, the two states, ruled by monarchs, maintained a cordial relationship. Again, in the 13th century, Mongolia invaded Myanmar as a result of a series of clashes along the shared border, which resulted in a 15-year occupation until a truce was reached. Myanmar experienced another invasion in the 14th century, which also ended with peaceful reconciliation. Over the years, both states witnessed minor conflicts until the 18th century, which marks the "last round of conflict" between the two sovereign states (Than, 2003). Between 1765 and 1769, the Konbaung dynasty fought off four Chinese invasions to Myanmar, eventually resulting in a peaceful treaty in December 1769 (Than, 2003). Since then, both sovereign states have enjoyed a cordial bilateral relationship through the "regular exchange of letters and visits" until 1874, when the British occupied and colonized the Myanmar kingdom (Than, 2003).

After gaining independence from the British kingdom in 1948, Myanmar recognized and welcomed the newly established People's Republic of China in 1949 (Than, 2003). Today, China is Myanmar's biggest investor and trading partner. This was not only as a result of China's rise as an economic superpower and Myanmar's dynamic socioeconomic development, but also due to a post-socialist economic transformation that has been occurring in both countries (Bolesta, 2018). In fact, Myanmar has strived to build its economy and model of development based on China's "with its closed political system, limited economic liberalization, state interventionism and heavy regulatory regime, as well as with its industrial policy" (Bolesta, 2018). Myanmar's economic liberalization in 1988 introduced new economic cooperation between the two countries.

What further strengthened the economic ties between Myanmar and China was the first series of international sanctions that the West imposed on Myanmar due to their human rights violations in 1988. The political and economic isolation led Myanmar to strengthen its economic ties with China (Bolesta, 2018). Similarly, in the 1950s, when the United States imposed containment policy against China, Myanmar stepped up to support its neighbor. For example, Myanmar opened up an international air route to

China so that China could continue its trade with Asia. When the UN put an embargo on China, Myanmar exported rubber despite criticism from the Western world (Huang, 2015). It can be argued that Myanmar continued its support for China to maintain "long-term stable relationship and to ensure the continuing gain of national interests, including survival and security" (Huang, 2015).

Three reasons were identified to explain why China also fostered a strong bilateral relationship with Myanmar. First, China reasoned that it is always beneficial to have a friendly neighboring country that is also dependent on China through economic interactions. Second, Myanmar has vast amount of natural resources, which can be accessed by China for its national development. And third, Myanmar is vital to China's transit system for transferring energy and natural resources from Africa and the Middle East, as well as exports to Europe, Africa, and the Middle East. As such, strong ties with Myanmar would further reinforce China's economic presence regionally and globally (Bolesta, 2018). As Andrzej Bolesta (2018) argues, "Transit through Myanmar makes the journey shorter and allows for the avoidance of the potentially politically unstable and heavily contested waters of the Malacca Strait and South China Sea".

Even during the transition period toward democracy, Myanmar enjoys a close bilateral relationship with China. The current government, National League for Democracy (NLD), under Aung Sun Suu Kyi, has implemented the "Letpadaung mining project, re-opened the China–Myanmar oil pipeline, and signed agreements on constructing a deep-water port in Kyaukpyu and established a China–Myanmar border economic cooperation zone" (Peng, 2018). In 2016, China was responsible for investing around US$18.4 billion in Myanmar, which is 31% of all foreign investments (Bolesta, 2018). In March 2016, the Government of Myanmar and PetroChina signed a deal that "allow[s] the Chinese energy company to import oil via the Bay of Bengal and pump it through a pipeline to supply a 260,000-barrel-per-day refinery in Yunnan province" (Bolesta, 2018). On September 9, 2018, China and Myanmar signed an MOU to finalize the CMEC, which is part of China's grand project, the BRI (Lwin, 2018; Peng, 2018). The corridor will connect both countries from China's Yunnan province to Myanmar's Mandalay, Yangon New City, and Kyaukpyu Special Economic Zone (Peng, 2018). In fact, the Kyaukpyu Special Economic Zone, which includes the deep-water port, is located in the west of Rakhine state, from where Rohingya Muslims are fleeing. Chinese development in Kyaukpyu will cost as much as US$7.3 billion, whereas the China–Myanmar oil pipeline going through Rakhine state to Yunnan province cost about US$2.45 billion (Reuters, 2017). As reported by Reuters, the pipeline is owned by "the China National Petroleum Corporation (51%) and Myanmar

Oil and Gas Enterprise . . . designed to carry 22 million tons of oil, up from 13 million tons currently, and up to 12 billion cubic meters of natural gas per year" (Reuters, 2017). In addition to supporting China's BRI project, Myanmar has been receptive to China's investment in other sectors such as banking, real estate, energy and natural resources, and so on (Bolesta, 2018).

In addition to China's investment and other economic assistance, Myanmar is also getting political support from China with the Rohingya crisis (Peng, 2018). For instance, China has been boycotting the UNSC resolution that would force the Government of Myanmar to work with the UN in addressing the Rohingya refugee crisis (Nichols, 2018). The resolution aims to put a timeline on Myanmar allowing the return of more than 700,000 Rohingya Muslim refugees from neighboring Bangladesh and addressing accountability (Nichols, 2018). China even went as far as to exercise its veto power at the UNSC when the Security Council called for action against Myanmar's military commanders by referring them to the ICC for ordering indiscriminate attacks and genocide on the Rohingya Muslims in Myanmar (Chin, 2018). In fact, China also "proposed the 'three-phase' plan for solving the Rohingya issue and facilitated a dialogue between Myanmar and Bangladesh regarding the repatriation of Rohingya refugees" (Peng, 2018). The three-phase plan consists of a cease-fire and then a bilateral dialogue to finalize a solution, and the third and final phase will consist of a long-term solution that will include repatriation (Ruwitch & Perry, 2017).

According to Yun Sun, from the Washington-based Stimson Center, China views the Rohingya crisis as an opportunity for bringing Myanmar into its sphere (Chin, 2018). As the West is not only retreating from but criticizing the Government of Myanmar, China has stepped in as Myanmar's "friend" (Chin, 2018). Both countries are benefitting from this bilateral relationship – China due to its access to Myanmar's energy and natural resources and Myanmar's support of China's multibillion-dollar BRI project (Bolesta, 2018; Chin, 2018); on the other hand, Myanmar is benefitting from China's immense economic assistance during its time of economic isolation and political support over the Rohingya crisis.

Role of ASEAN in the Rohingya crisis

Myanmar became a member of the ASEAN on July 3, 1997. Even though ASEAN was established in 1967, it admitted Myanmar, then known as Burma, late due to pressure from Western governments: "the objective was to force Burma's rulers, then known as the SLORC – State Law and Order Restoration Council, which changed its name to State Peace and Development Council in late 1997 to make democratic concessions by means of economic sanctions and by keeping diplomatic contacts at a minimum"

The Rohingya crisis and geopolitics 45

(Cribb, 1998). Regardless, Myanmar became a member of ASEAN in 1997. Given that the Rohingya refugee crisis has become "a full-blown humanitarian crisis" with regional implications – as it spilled over the border in Bangladesh and other neighboring countries – ASEAN is expected to take a stance regarding the crisis (Shivakoti, 2017). In fact, the Rohingya crisis highlighted the limitation of ASEAN with a "lack of a political and legal framework to deal with issues related to refugees" (Shivakoti, 2017). Among the ten member ASEAN nations, only the Philippines and Cambodia are signatories of the 1951 Convention Relating to the Status of Refugees or its 1967 Protocol (Shivakoti, 2017). As such, ASEAN as a regional organization lacks the structure to force the member states, including Myanmar, to comply with the repatriation and protection of the Rohingya refugees.

Another reason why ASEAN cannot force the Government of Myanmar to comply with the repatriation of the Rohingya refugees is due to the clause of "non-interference in the internal affairs of ASEAN Member States" (Shivakoti, 2017). Nevertheless, that has not stopped ASEAN members from speaking out individually against the crimes of the Government of Myanmar (Doody, 2018). Muslim-majority countries, such as Malaysia and Indonesia, have become more vocal about the protection and repatriation of the Rohingya Muslims and highlighted it as a regional problem. The Malaysian prime minister even went as far as to demand that "justice to be brought to the perpetrators of the Rohingya crisis, and said that the repatriation process should include citizenship" (Heijmans, 2019). However, the other countries have maintained their nonintervention policy by not putting pressure on Myanmar. These differing positions regarding the Rohingya crisis have resulted in tensions among ASEAN members. Myanmar and its allies in ASEAN are not committed to finding a long-term resolution to the conflict due to narrow gains.

The search for a sustainable solution of the Rohingya crisis: a policy conundrum for Bangladesh

Even with formal diplomatic relationships between them, both Bangladesh and Myanmar have made little headway in finding a solution to the Rohingya refugee crisis. Bangladesh simply lacks the resources and infrastructure needed to cope with and provide for the Rohingya refugees. Currently, approximately 1.2 million refugees have been provided shelter in a series of camps in Cox Bazar (Storey, 2017; UNB Dhaka, 2019). The Government of Bangladesh has been encouraging the locals in the Cox Bazar region of Bangladesh to welcome the refugees (Alam, 2017). However, it should be noted that Bangladesh is not a state member to the 1951 UN Refugee Convention, and as such, Bangladesh has no obligation to support the Rohingya refugees. In fact, providing shelter to the refugees is a temporary solution, and to reach a permanent solution, Myanmar has to come to the table as well. Bangladesh has urged the international community to ramp up pressure on Myanmar so that it creates a congenial environment for the earliest repatriation of displaced Rohingyas with safety and dignity. Bangladesh and Myanmar reached a repatriation deal on November 23, 2017, and again on January 16, 2018. Both states reached a "physical arrangement" deal that aimed to repatriate the Rohingya refugees within two years; however, both these agreements have proved to be ineffective (Uddin Ahmed, 2018).

Despite the multidimensional consequences of the Rohingya refugee crisis, Bangladesh has little sway over Myanmar. The European Union, the United States, the United Kingdom, France, and other Western and Muslim countries have been vocal critics of the Government of Myanmar's handling of the Rohingya crisis, even going as far as to sanction and put an embargo on Myanmar (Uddin Ahmed, 2018). But Myanmar is able to get away with international sanctions and embargos due to China, Russia, and India's support. As mentioned already, Myanmar is geopolitically important to China and India because it provides both countries a way to "connect their landlocked eastern regions to the Bay of Bengal and to the fast growing Southeast Asia" (Uddin Ahmed, 2018). Binoda Mishra, foreign policy analyst of India, was quoted regarding Myanmar's geopolitical interest: "[b]oth India and China engage the Burmese military as much as the civilian government because the country is key to India's Act East policy and China's Belt and Road Initiative" (Uddin Ahmed, 2018). In fact, both countries have also made considerable economic investments in Myanmar, particularly the Rakhine region, because it is the key route to the Bay of Bengal (Uddin Ahmed, 2018). As of mid-2017, India invested about US$1.75 billion in Myanmar in grants and credit, whereas China invested about US$18.53 billion in Myanmar (Uddin Ahmed, 2018). Given the huge support from two of the rising giants in Asia, India and China, Bangladesh cannot put much pressure on Myanmar for Rohingya repatriation.

One of the ways for Bangladesh to solve its dispute with Myanmar over the Rohingya crisis is by reaching out to China and/or India. The foreign minister of Bangladesh reached out to China several times for their "'strong support' so that Myanmar moves in the 'right direction' for resolving the Rohingya crisis" (bdnews24.com, 2019). In response, China stated that "it is willing to play a constructive role to realize repatriation of the displaced people and will maintain close communication with Bangladesh and Myanmar to find a practical solution to the crisis" (bdnews24.com, 2019).

In July 2019, Bangladesh stated to the UN that it is not able to absorb any more Rohingya refugees fleeing the persecution and genocide by the Government of Myanmar. The Bangladesh foreign secretary openly expressed his frustration with the UN and Western countries for not taking a more active role in solving the Rohingya crisis (Ellis-Petersen, 2019). Additionally, the foreign secretary also denounced "Myanmar's failure to take steps towards repatriation of Rohingya" (Ellis-Petersen, 2019). Despite an effort to repatriate Rohingyas in the Rakhine state of Myanmar, he emphasized that "not a single Rohingya has volunteered to return to Rakhine due to the absence of a conducive environment there" (Ellis-Petersen, 2019). With little sway over Myanmar, the Bangladeshi state has reached out to the international community, including China, to find a concrete solution to the Rohingya refugee crisis. But all these diplomatic efforts have not changed the reality of Rakhine state and the fate of the Rohingya community.

Concluding remarks

The Rohingya crisis shows the contentious role of geopolitics ignoring humanity at the cost of economic and strategic gains of regional powers. Both China and India are keen to keep their warm relationship with Myanmar's regime and are not ready to put any pressure on the regime for solving the crisis. The Government of Myanmar knows it has friends, like China and Russia, who will block any move of putting serious pressure against it in UNSC. On the other hand, Bangladesh is lacking any strong or visible support from regional or global powers. Until now, most of the international resolutions on this issue have been ineffective in terms of achieving the goal of ensuring a safe and dignified repatriation of Rohingya refugees. When this crisis emerged in 2017, it was a shock and surprise for the Government of Bangladesh. The regime in Bangladesh had no idea about or preparation for this sudden influx. But it managed the initial shock in an efficient manner. Because the civil and military administration of Bangladesh has been quite experienced and competent in disaster management, relief, and rehabilitation for a long period of time, it was not difficult for the government to arrange shelter and other daily necessities for the Rohingya refugees. The role of the international community in the relief and rehabilitation program was also commendable.

In terms of its foreign policy, Bangladesh initially took a soft stand against Myanmar's regime. The government was struggling to find the a right strategy and partnership to put pressure on Myanmar for ensuring repatriation. They were overdependent on China to negotiate with Myanmar on this issue. It is still to be observed whether the China-driven solution of this crisis can ensure the sustainable repatriation of the Rohingyas. The process of repatriation of the Rohingyas must be done with their consent, assured safety, and protection, and carried out in a dignified manner. Most importantly, is must be guaranteed that they are not going to detention camps but to their homes and villages, and are given their rights to Myanmar citizenship. In sum, it is essential that this solution is sustainable (Albar, 2019).

The Rohingya crisis is a grave concern for Bangladesh. It currently hosts more than 1.2 million Rohingya, who have been forcibly displaced and subjected to genocide, ethnic cleansing, and systematic discrimination for years in Rakhine, Myanmar. Despite international agreements/instruments such as the Responsibility to Protect (R2P) and the UN, regional bodies and major powers have failed to play their collective roles to protect these ill-fated people. Failure in implementation of the Anan Commission Report, the UN Special Investigation Report, the UNHRC Report, the Special Rapporteur Report, and the Gert Rosenthal Report (2010–2018) is a manifestation of the systematic weakness of the UN. In all the reports, the UN and other international bodies seemed to tolerate and become subservient to Yangon's interest and hence not to the interests of the Rohingyas. Myanmar was unwilling to make even a basic commitment to a foundation for any partnership because it was confident that no implications or consequences would result from its nonaction (Albar, 2019).

The Rohingyas are one of the most persecuted ethnic minorities in the present world. Although the focus of the crisis seems to be on the threat for the host country, this could affect regional peace, security, and stability in the rest of South and Southeast Asia. Despite being a small economy, for its commitment to global peace and security, Bangladesh has extended its wholehearted assistance to millions of ill-fated people fleeing from death. Despite the humanitarian assistance provided by the international community, the country has been providing key financial and logistical assistance for their basic needs. Bangladesh required US$1,211 million in one fiscal year (2018–2019) to support the Rohingyas (Khatun & Kamruzzaman, 2018). Nevertheless, Bangladesh has been facing numerous development challenges of its own and might not be able to support over a million extra people for an indefinite period of time. The presence of a huge number of frustrated Rohingyas in confined, makeshift camps without basic rights or needs addressed has already become a socioeconomic concern for Bangladesh. There has been a demographic imbalance in the subdistrict of Ukhia and Tekhnaf, where the number of Rohingyas exceeds the entire population combined. Thus, this grave humanitarian crisis requires urgent attention from national, regional, and international communities and stakeholders for effective repatriation from Bangladesh. The Rohingya crisis is a complicated humanitarian and geopolitical concern. Therefore, the governments of Bangladesh and Myanmar and international agencies need to ensure that a proper balance is maintained between the humanitarian concerns and the geopolitical interests of regional and global powers while designing a practical strategy of repatriation.

References

Alam, M. (2017). *The Rohingya crisis and the risk to American geopolitical interests – Just security.* Retrieved from www.justsecurity.org/45410/rohingya-crisis-risk-american-geopolitical-interests/

Albar, S. H. (2019). Key note paper of the International Conference on Rohingya Crisis in Bangladesh: Challenges and Sustainable Solutions, held at North South University, July 2019. Retrieved from http://institutions.northsouth.edu/rohingya-2019/wp-content/uploads/2019/07/EXECUTIVE-SUMMARY_21-July.pdf

bdnews24.com (2019). Bangladesh seeks China's support to nudge Myanmar on Rohingya issue. Retrieved from https://bdnews24.com/bangladesh/2019/01/27/bangladesh-seeks-chinas-support-to-nudge-myanmar-on-rohingya-issue

Berryman, J. (2012). Geopolitics and Russian foreign policy. *International Politics, 49*(4), 530–544. https://doi.org/10.1057/ip.2012.15

Bhattacharya, P. (2018). India's bid for enhanced regional role. *The Daily Star.* Retrieved from www.thedailystar.net/opinion/global-affairs/news/indias-bid-enhanced-regional-role-1678303

Bissinger, J. (2010). The maritime boundary dispute between Bangladesh and Myanmar: Motivations, potential solutions, and implications. *Asia Policy, 10*, 103–142. Retrieved from www.jstor.org/stable/24905004.

Bolesta, A. (2018). Myanmar-China peculiar relationship: Trade, investment and the model of development. *Journal of International Studies, 11*(2), 23–36. https://doi.org/10.14254/2071-8330.2018/11-2/2

Calamur, K. (2017). The misunderstood roots of Burma's Rohingya crisis. *The Atlantic website.* Retrieved June 12, 2019, from www.theatlantic.com/international/archive/2017/09/rohingyas-burma/540513/

Chatzky, A., & McBride, J. (2019). China's massive belt and road initiative. *Council on Foreign Relations.* Retrieved from www.cfr.org/backgrounder/chinas-massive-belt-and-road-initiative

Chaudhary, D. R. (2019). India all set to take over ops in Myanmar's Sittwe Port after Chabahar. *Economic Times India.* Retrieved from https://economictimes.indiatimes.com/articleshow/67437859.cms?from=mdr&utm_source=contentofinterest&utm_medium=text&utm_campaign=cppst

Chin, J. (2018). Call for Rohingya genocide prosecution to deepen China's support of Myanmar. *Wall Street Journal.* Retrieved from www.wsj.com/articles/call-for-rohingya-genocide-prosecution-lets-china-rush-to-myanmars-rescue-1535536804

Cribb, R. (1998). Burma's entry in to ASEAN: Background and implications. *Asian Perspective, 22*(3), 49–62. Retrieved from www.jstor.org/stable/42704181

Doody, J. (2018). Can ASEAN economic integration succeed? *The Diplomat.* Retrieved from https://thediplomat.com/2018/04/can-asean-economic-integration-succeed/

Ellis-Petersen, H. (2019). Rohingya crisis: Bangladesh says it will not accept any more Myanmar refugees. *The Guardian.* Retrieved from www.theguardian.com/world/2019/mar/01/rohingya-crisis-bangladesh-says-it-will-not-accept-any-more-myanmar-refugees

Engh, S. (2016). Indian's Myanmar policy and the "Sino-Indian Great Game". *Asian Affairs, 47*(1), 32–58. https://doi-org.proxy.lib.sfu.ca/10.1080/03068374.2015.11 30307

Ethirajan, A. (2015). The Burmese Indians who never went home. *BBC News*. Retrieved from https://www.bbc.com/news/world-asia-33973982

Haque, M. M. (2015). Multicultural society in Burma: How it failed to accommodate the Rohingya identity. *Journal of Language and Culture, 34*(2). Retrieved from https://pdfs.semanticscholar.org/ac4f/743ce450e2f4705ee88b28ad8b5f2bc6b421.pdf?_ga=2.33943841.1832829282.1586698742-1176010830.1586698742

Heijmans, P. (2019). ASEAN leaders hold off from demanding citizenship for Rohingyas. *Bloomberg*. Retrieved from www.bloomberg.com/news/articles/2019-06-23/asean-leaders-hold-off-from-demanding-citizenship-for-rohingyas

Htwe, C. M. (2017). Rohingyas, Belt and Road, Kaladan – the future of Rakhine's economy. *The Myanmar Times*. Retrieved from https://www.mmtimes.com/news/rohingyas-belt-and-road-kaladan-future-rakhines-economy.html

Huang, C.-C. (2015). Balance of relationship: The essence of Myanmar's China policy. *The Pacific Review, 28*(2), 189–210. https://doi.org/10.1080/09512748.2 014.995122

Kallol, A. S. (2017). Bangladesh-Myanmar trade remains healthy amidst Rohingya crisis. *Dhaka Tribune*. Retrieved from www.dhakatribune.com/business/commerce/2017/10/17/bangladesh-myanmar-trade-remains-healthy-amidst-rohingya-crisis

Kaplan, R. D. (2010). The geography of Chinese power: How far can Beijing reach on land and at sea? *Foreign Affairs, 89*(3), 22–41. Retrieved from www.jstor.org/stable/25680913

Khatun, F., & Kamruzzaman, M. (2018). *Fiscal implications of Rohingya crisis for Bangladesh*. CPD Working paper 120. Dhaka: Centre for Policy Dialogue.

Lee, L. (2014). Myanmar's transition to democracy: New opportunities or obstacles for India? *Contemporary Southeast Asia: A Journal of International and Strategic Affairs, 36*(2), 290–316. Retrieved from http://muse.jhu.edu/article/555004

Lwin, N. (2018). Gov't Signs MoU with Beijing to Build China-Myanmar economic corridor. *The Irrawaddy*. Retrieved from www.irrawaddy.com/news/burma/govt-signs-mou-beijing-build-china-myanmar-economic-corridor.html

Nichols, M. (2018). U.N. Security council mulls Myanmar action; Russia, China boycott . . . *Reuters*. Retrieved from www.reuters.com/article/us-myanmar-rohingya-un-idUSKBN1OG2CJ

Nolte, D. (2010). How to compare regional powers: Analytical concepts and research topics. *Review of International Studies, 36*(4), 881–901. https://doi.org/10.1017/S026021051000135X

Parnini, S. N., Othman, M. R., & Ghazali, A. S. (2013). The Rohingya refugee crisis and Bangladesh-Myanmar relations. *Asian and Pacific Migration Journal, 22*(1), 133–146. https://doi.org/10.1177/011719681302200107

Patten, C. (2013). Geopolitical theory. *Presentation*. Retrieved from www.slideshare.net/cindipatten/geopolitical-theory

Peng, N. (2018). *China and Myanmar's budding relationship*. Retrieved June 14, 2019, from East Asia Forum website www.eastasiaforum.org/2018/08/24/china-and-myanmars-budding-relationship/
PIB, The Hindu. (2019). *Prelim Bits 20-03-2019*. IAS Parliament. Retrieved from https://www.iasparliament.com/current-affairs/prelim-bits-20-03-2019#:~:text=Sittwe%20port%20is%20located%20at,Mizoram%20in%20north%2Deastern%20India.&text=This%20project%20will%20reduce%20distance,also%20known%20as%20Chicken's%20Neck.
Ramya, P. S. (2018). Myanmar's approach to India. *The Diplomat*. Retrieved from https://thediplomat.com/2018/03/myanmars-approach-to-india/
Rashid, H. U. (2019). Bangladesh-Myanmar relations: An overview. *Dhaka Courier*. Retrieved from www.dhakacourier.com.bd/news/Column/Bangladesh-Myanmar-Relations:-An-Overview/953
Reuters. (2017). China and its economic stake in Rakhine. *Dhaka Tribune*. Retrieved from www.dhakatribune.com/world/south-asia/2017/09/24/economic-stakes-china-rakhine/
Ruwitch, J., & Perry, M. (2017). China proposed three-phase plan for Rohingya issue. *Reuters*. Retrieved from www.reuters.com/article/us-china-myanmar-rohingya-idUSKBN1DK00I
Shivakoti, R. (2017). ASEAN's role in the Rohingya refugee crisis. *Forced Migration Review*, 56, 3.
Storey, H. (2017). *Proxies: The Brutal Geopolitics of the Rohingya Crisis*. Foreign Brief. Retrieved from https://www.foreignbrief.com/asia-pacific/south-east-asia/proxies-geopolitics-rohingya-crisis/
Than, T. M. M. (2003). Myanmar and China: A special relationship? *Southeast Asian Affairs, 2003*(1), 189–210. Retrieved from https://muse.jhu.edu/article/400084/summary
Trivedi, S. (2018). India and Myanmar share cultural, historical links. *The Myanmar Times*. Retrieved from https://www.mmtimes.com/news/india-and-myanmar-share-cultural-historical-links.html
Uddin Ahmed, K. (2018). The geo-politics of Rohingya crisis. *The Financial Express*.
UNB Dhaka. (2019). Mount pressure on Myanmar: Bangladesh to diplomats. *The Daily Star*. Retrieved from www.thedailystar.net/rohingya-crisis/news/fm-briefing-diplomats-focus-rohingya-issue-1755889
Wu, Z. (2018). Classical geopolitics, realism and the balance of power theory. *Journal of Strategic Studies, 41*(6), 786–823. https://doi.org/10.1080/01402390.2017.1379398
Yhome, K. (2009). *India-Myanmar Relations (1998–2008): A Decade of Redefining Bilateral Relations* [Research]. Observer Research Foundation. Retrieved from https://www.orfonline.org/research/india-myanmar-relations-1998-2008-a-decade-of-redefining-bilateral-relations/

3 A future for the Rohingya in Myanmar

Md. Mahbubul Haque

The Rohingya Muslim crisis started in the late 18th century. It has changed its shape and nature since then, but has mostly focused on Rohingya ethnicity and religion. In Myanmar's post-independence history, the Rohingya and other ethnic minorities have been in conflict with the Rangoon-based central government. This became more pronounced when General Ne Win took power in 1962. From that time onward, the entire machinery of the government adopted a series of policies against Rohingya existence in Myanmar. The UN has called the Rohingya "one of the most persecuted minorities on earth" (Aljazeera, 2012). It can be strongly argued that the Rohingya community has endured progressive intensification of discrimination over the past 58 years. The Rohingya people have experienced difficulties in obtaining citizenship since the enactment of the 1982 Citizenship Law in Myanmar despite the fact that their separate identity was recognized by the democratic government of Premier U Nu (1948–1962). The Government of Myanmar consistently claims that the Rohingya Muslim minority migrated to Myanmar (formerly Burma) during the colonial period. Thus they failed to meet the criteria of so-called indigenous ethnic group of Myanmar. Furthermore, the Myanmar military alleged that the Rohingya Muslims are involved with separatist movements that threaten to destabilize Myanmar. Since the early days of independence, major ethnic minorities have been struggling to establish their rights under the union, and at the present time Kachin, Karen, Shan, and even Rakhine rebel groups often clash with the Myanmar army. The Government of Myanmar has conducted a number of military operations against the Rohingya Muslims in Rakhine state in the name of national security.

There are many historical documents that bear witness to the fact that the Indo-Aryan Rohingya have a long presence in Myanmar, particularly in the Arakan region. During colonial times, there were no restrictions on movement of people between Bengal or Arakan and the rest of the present nation-state of Myanmar. Moreover, cross-border contacts between Chittagong and

Arakan were common. It is not unlikely that the Chittagongian settlements in the border areas merged with the local Rohingya settlements in Myanmar.

In this chapter I argue that the ethnic Muslim minority Rohingyas have been completely deprived and are unwanted due to their race and ethnicity. This attitude was reflected recently in the Myanmar administration when General Min Aung Hlaing referred to the ongoing military operation in Rakhine state as "unfinished business from 1942", a reference to the time when it was a shifting front line in the battles between British and Japanese forces (Head, 2017). Rohingya Muslims and Burman-Rakhine Buddhists largely supported opposing sides in that war, and there were massacres by militias on both sides and large population movements. These historical incidents have created mistrust and have given legacy to this long-standing crisis.

The Rohingya minority had strong involvement in the government before and after the independence of Burma. This is evident in the 2010–2015 parliament, in which three Rohingya Members of Parliament (MPs) were elected from the Muslim-dominated constituency in Rakhine state (Haque, 2017b). However, the situation changed for Rohingya and other Muslim ethnic minorities after the 2012 Buddhist-Muslim riots. The unrest was triggered by the rape and murder of a Rakhine Buddhist girl during the last week of May 2012, allegedly by three Muslims, and the lynching of ten Muslims on June 3 in apparent retaliation. On June 8, 2012, the Rohingyas started to protest during Friday's prayers in Maungdaw township. More than a dozen residents were killed after police started firing. President Thein Sein announced a state of emergency in western Myanmar on June 10, following deadly clashes between Buddhists and Muslims. The 2012 communal riots were a series of conflicts primarily between ethnic Rakhine Buddhists and Rohingya Muslims in northern Rakhine state, although by October Muslims of all ethnicities were targeted. Subsequently, major political parties failed to nominate any Muslim candidate in the 2015 parliamentary election. Most recently the Government of Myanmar launched a major military operation against Rohingya civilians using the pretext of hunting down militants who attacked government buildings, including police stations, on August 25, 2017. Since the operation, more than a million Rohingya refugees, most of whom fled genocidal attacks by the Myanmar military in 2016 and 2017, live in overcrowded temporary shelters in Cox's Bazar District, Bangladesh (Photo 3.1 and 3.4). Genocide is still taking place against Rohingya Muslims remaining in Myanmar, and the government is increasingly demonstrating that it has no interest in establishing a fully functioning democracy, according to UN investigators (Lederer, 2018).

Irrespective of international pressures, the main institutions of the Government of Myanmar, military, major political parties, media, and radical Buddhist monks will not accept the Rohingya as citizens. Their speeches

54 Md. Mahbubul Haque

Photo 3.1 Displaced Rohingya temporary shelters made from bamboo cane and filthy plastic, Cox's Bazar, Bangladesh

online and to party cadre have demonstrated a hatred toward the Rohingya. There are two main reasons behind this – ethnocentrism and Islamophobia – and both will be addressed later in the chapter. In this dangerous context for Rohingya, it is important to hear the views of Rohingya on how they could coexist in Myanmar society despite years of hatred and insecurity. This chapter is based on community leaders' ethnographic interviews and documentary analysis. It explores the views of the Rohingya community both at home and abroad and will focus on how they fit within the Myanmar mainstream political process.

Race and ethnocentrism

Denial of access to citizenship is not a new issue in modern nation-states. It can be argued that race and ethnicity are the major factors behind the denial of citizenship. After the collapse of the Soviet Union and Eastern Europe, many newly independent states faced this complexity. A sizeable number of Russians are now becoming second-class citizens in the former Soviet states. Disintegration problems are not only confined to Europe. In Asia and the Middle East, where nationality is primarily conferred on a *jus sanguinis* basis, there is a strong trend developed over the decades to denial or deprivation of nationality in the name of race superiority. Racism takes many forms and occurs in many places. It includes prejudice, discrimination, or hatred directed at someone because of color, ethnicity, or national origin.

People often associate racism with acts of abuse or harassment. It is noted that in Myanmar "Kalar" or "Kala"[1] is a derogatory and racist term widely used to refer to persons of Muslim or South Asian descent. In official and unofficial communications, authorities still commonly refer to Rohingya as Bengali, so-called Rohingya, or the derogatory form "Kalar" (Fortify Rights, 2014, p. 16). The International Convention on the Elimination of All Forms of Racial Discrimination, Article 1, specifically mentions racial discrimination encompasses actions "based on race, colour, descent or national or ethnic origin" (OHCHR, 1965). It is one of the major consensuses of international human rights law that no one shall be deprived due to his or her "race" identity. But it does not mean that racist attitudes and racism have been abolished from modern societies.

Racial superiority or purity can lead to racial hatred. However, not all racism comes from hatred. Some of it can come from fear and anxiety. People may worry that some groups pose a threat, whether to the safety of the community or to national identity. "For political purposes 'race' is not so much a biological phenomenon as a social myth. The myth of 'race' has created an enormous amount of human and social damage" (Haque, 2014, p. 60). In recent years it has taken a heavy toll in human lives and caused untold suffering. It still prevents the normal development of millions of human beings and deprives civilization of the effective cooperation of productive minds. The biological differences among ethnic groups are now disregarded from the standpoint of social acceptance. The social sciences have come to reject biological notions of race in favor of an approach that regards race as a social concept. In the 19th century, "Max Weber discounted biological explanations for racial conflict and instead highlighted the social and political factors which engendered such conflict" (Omi & Winant, 1994, p. 11). It is interpreted many ways in different countries. Scientists are still arguing that complexion is not made by society or a particular tribe. All human complexions are influenced by geographic location and the habits of individuals. It is not related to the boundary of a present nation-state. Racial diversity or similarity does not link with a state boundary.

A Weberian analysis leads to a rejection of the Government of Myanmar's arguments on race interpretation; rather, it can be stated that the problem is that Rohingyas have a different culture and religious identity that is not welcome in the present Myanmar nation-state. Race is the major factor to decide Myanmar citizenship under the 1982 law. It is well-known that Rohingyas' Indo-Aryan complexion makes them ineligible for Myanmar citizenship. This view has also been reflected through the Myanmar political leaders' and civil society's conversation at different times.[2] There is no justification to exclude the Rohingya because of their different ethnicity and race; rather, it is ethnocentrism against the Rohingya Muslim minority in Myanmar.

The systematic use of the concept of ethnicity is relatively recent in sociology and social anthropology. Ethnicity means a group of people who derive from the same ancestry, history, language or dialect, sort of ideology, religion, cuisine, custom, and physical appearance. An ethnic group is a distinct category of the population in a larger society whose culture is usually different from that group. The terms "race", "religion", "language", and "territory" each refer to potentially observable social attributes (albeit in graduations), whereas the term "ethnicity" indicates a form of collective consciousness that employs those attributes as the symbolic markers for bounded communities of assumed common ancestry, thereby attributing to them moral significance (Brown, 2007, p. 17).

Historically people have often expressed prejudice toward and discriminated against others on the basis of ethnicity. Leo Kuper (1974) argues that the ethnocentric attitude is not a new phenomenon in the modern nation-state. Ancient Greek history expressed this attitude, such as a "barbarian" is not entitled to some rights. It is originated from a so-called ethnocentric attitude. Ethnocentrism is the tendency to believe that one particular ethnic or cultural group is more important and all other groups are treated as less important. The term "ethnocentrism" was identified by William G. Summer upon observing the tendency for people to differentiate between the in-group and others. He described it as often leading to pride, vanity, beliefs of one's own group's superiority, and contempt of outsiders (cited in Andersen & Taylor, 2006). For this study's purpose, it is important to identify how ethnocentrism involves victimization of the Rohingyas' identity in the present nation-state of Myanmar.

Apart from ethnocentrism, some other factors have played important roles to instigate this crisis. Psychoanalyst Vamik Volkan (2008) comments how "large-group" identity can contribute to ultranationalism and influence conflict against an ethnic minority. The long-standing national and ethnic conflict is not merely a result of political, legal, or economic deprivation. It has "psychologized" contamination, with perceptions, thoughts, and emotions about national issues. Volkan provides many examples of political leaders having a psychological complexity that contributed to ethnic and nationalistic conflict in different countries. He provided examples from the destructive leadership of Slobodan Milošević and Radovan Karadzic in Serbia and Kosovo. In Myanmar's context, the Rohingya Muslim minority did not face many problems before General Ne Win introduced "the Burmese Way to Socialism".[3] Many scholars described this program as xenophobic, superstitious, and an "abject failure", turning one of the most prosperous countries in Asia into one of the world's poorest (William, 1993). General

A future for the Rohingya in Myanmar 57

Ne Win had strong objectives to rule the country: a national identity constructed by the majority Burman; the military's direct involvement in politics; and disparate action against ethnic minorities and political dissidents.

Volkan (2008) argues that group leadership often works to support the leaders' political ambitions, and conscious and unconscious psychological needs can encourage a process of demonization and dehumanization of the group's enemies. These phenomena are quite similar in the Myanmar context. The dictator Ne Win followed an aggressive racial policy that affected every minority group. The whole state conducted operations against those of Indian origin, and it should be mentioned that thousands of South Asians and a few Chinese left the country without any property or compensation. "Between 1962 and 1964, more than 300,000 Indians were forced out of Burma" (Daniyal, 2017). The cruelest policy was the 1982 Citizenship Law. It was created as a strict racial definition of citizenship. Through this law, Ne Win tried to establish so-called pure blood supremacy in the name of indigenous ethnicity. As a result, ethnic Muslim minority Rohingya became *de jure* stateless from their ancestors. Due to statelessness, many of the Rohingya have fled into neighboring countries. The vast majority have sought refuge in Bangladesh, while a sizable number have gone to Malaysia and Thailand. Their legal status is also questionable in those countries where they are residing for more than decades (Photo 3.2 and 3.3).

Photo 3.2 Rohingya education center in Terengganu State, Malaysia

Islamophobia and Rohingyaphobia

Islamophobia is a common word in recent political discourse, and it is clear that this term is widely associated with Muslims all over the world. Some Western writers have frequently used the term and have tried to identify Islam as an inherently fundamentalist religion whose followers have nothing in common with other cultures. First, as a term, "Islamophobia" was discussed in the UK-based left-wing think tank Runnymede Trust report in 1991. Runnymede Trust defined it as "unfounded hostility towards Muslims, and therefore fear or dislike of all or most Muslims" (Musaji, 2016). It was coined in the UK and greater European context to address the xenophobia framework. Islamophobia is not confined to the West and at present has gradually spread all over the world. There is a strong perception that the terrorist organizations Al-Qaeda and ISIS have exploited protracted conflicts across the Muslim world to further their agendas, including in areas that are under the sovereignty of capable states but where central government authority is weak. After 9/11, it has been easier for the anti-Muslim camp to establish their claim that Muslims are closely connected with terrorist groups.

Although it has no strong basis in Rohingya society, a few leaders dream to establish a Sharia state in the Muslim-dominated northern part of Rakhine state.[4] Even the recently formed insurgent group Arakan Rohingya Salvation Army (ARSA) strongly denied their involvement with any global Islamic movement. ARSA leader Ata Ullah stated that "we are fighting for our rights, and to try to get guns and ammunition from the Myanmar military, that's all" (cited in Head, 2017). Bangkok-based security analyst Anthony Davis commented on ARSA's activities and stated that "they do not have any substantive links with international jihadism, IS [Islamic State] or al-Qaeda. They see their struggle as regaining rights for Rohingya inside Rakhine State. They are neither separatists, nor jihadists" (cited in Head, 2017).

Currently in Myanmar, Islam and Islamic culture are always projected in distorted forms through the media. Anti-Islamic propaganda became strong through social media, particularly after the violent Buddhist-Muslim conflict of 2012. Ashin Wirathu, a young monk, started the anti-Rohingya Muslim campaign. This fanatical movement, known as "969", has openly instigated riots and carried out a series of deadly incidents and massacres against Muslims all over Myanmar. "The 969 movement has picked up the Rakhine crisis issues to feed its own anti-Muslim discourse, but it was not bred in the Rakhine state" (Leider, 2017). The main objective of the 969 movement is to protect Buddhism and stop the expansion of Islam in predominantly Buddhist Myanmar. Wirathu has long been accused of inciting sectarian violence against Myanmar's Muslims, in particular the Rohingya community, through hate-filled, Islamophobic speeches. Wirathu has tried to justify his movement, for example, in conversation with journalist Peter Popham:

> We represent Burma's 135 ethnic groups. We are urging members of those ethnic groups not to follow the Muslim religion and not to sell anything to Muslims, and that includes paddy fields and houses. The reason is that we have to protect our religion. If we trade with the Muslims, they become rich: many Muslims have grown rich and have built big houses for themselves, and mosques, and slaughter houses, which are a problem for Buddhism. Muslims are now dominating the Burmese economy.
>
> (Popham, 2013)

Time magazine (July 2013 issue) criticized Wirathu's communal attitude. The Singapore-based newspaper *The Straits Times* (April 8, 2013) described his movement as a "Neo-Nazi" group in Myanmar with anti-Muslim sentiments. He was at the forefront of Myanmar's radical nationalist movement, and he supported the military crackdown on the Rohingya in August 2017 in Rakhine state. The situation changed for Wirathu after he made incendiary remarks about Aung San Suu Kyi. According to international media, the police confirmed that a warrant had been issued for Wirathu's arrest under Article 124(a) of the penal code. It covers sedition, defined as "attempts to bring into hatred or contempt, or excites or attempts to excite disaffection towards the government" (cited in Petersen, 2019). The charge carries a three-year prison sentence.

However, some Buddhist fundamentalist groups are targeting all Muslims together and instigating anti-Islamic propaganda. Arakan historian Jacques P. Leider (2017) recently opined, "the frictions in the Rakhine State are less about Islamophobia than Rohingya-Phobia". But Leider failed to establish evidence about Rohingyaphobia in current Myanmar political discourse. It is noted that the Muslim communities are not united, and some groups have different opinions regarding the Rohingya crisis. The Panthay Muslims, ethnically close to the Chinese community, are keen to gain official recognition for their ethnic group. It can be estimated that all Panthays hold full Myanmar citizenship and thus are less concerned about politics and consequences from the census than other groups in a more tenuous situation (Mullins & Aye, 2014). There are Indian-origin Muslims living mainly in Yangon and Mandalay. The Chulia Muslim and human rights activist Hossain Kader is concerned about the Rohingya issue, but at the same time he believes the democratic regime can resolve the long-standing conflict among the ethnic minorities, including the Rohingya.[5] This research has shown that most of the ethnic Muslim minorities do not want to fight against the government but rather to make sure of the status quo within the democratic regime. In the light of this discussion, it can be argued that newly invented Rohingyaphobia or Islamophobia are both used by the Myanmar ruling elites to try to legitimize their atrocities.

Rohingya in Arakan and the present nation-state of Myanmar

This historical discussion seeks to understand the whole scenario of the Rohingya from pre-colonization to present-day Myanmar. It is one of the most ethnically diverse and biggest countries of Southeast Asia. The present Myanmar state was integrated as a province of British India through the third Anglo-Burma War in 1824. After three Anglo-Burma Wars (1825, 1852, and 1885), Burma was conquered and transformed into a British colony. It is noted that after the first Anglo-Burma War, "the territories of Rakhine and Taninthary were absorbed into the administrative structures in the British India Company through its agents in Bengal" (Taylor, 2007, p. 73). Burma became an official colony of Britain on January 1, 1886. The British ruled Burma as a part of India, and after 1937 it was made a crown colony of Britain. The present nation-state of Myanmar is in a geographically unique position to connect three regions: South, Southeast, and East Asia.

The nature of Burmese society and religion, and the comparatively short period of its colonial experience, prevented the Burmese from integrating with the British Empire. From its early days of colonization, Burma saw a large number of Indian migrants trying to grasp opportunities in this resource-rich but underdeveloped and restive land. After the opening of the Suez Canal, the demand for Burmese rice grew, and vast tracts of land were opened up for cultivation. However, to prepare the new land for cultivation, farmers borrowed money from Indian moneylenders called *Chettiars*.[6] The civil service was largely staffed by Anglo-Burmese and Indians; Burmese were excluded almost entirely from military service, which was staffed primarily with Indians, Anglo-Burmese, Karens, and other minority groups. During the whole decade of the 1930s, the Burmese nationalist movement developed and showed its violent attitude against the Indian settlers.

An Indian family resident in Burma and former bureaucrat Nalini Ranjan Chakravarty stated that "an indiscriminate attack on Indians followed, on a scale very much larger than that witnessed in 1930 and 1931, including cold-blooded murders, grievous hurts, looting arson. The massacre and rioting soon spread throughout Burma. The total loss of lives and property never exactly evaluated" (1971, p. 158). It should be mentioned here that during the unrest, law enforcers and the government headed by Ba Maw were silent and did not take any action against the perpetrators. The governor appointed a committee toward the end of September 1938 to identify the causes of the riots and reasons for the ineffectiveness of the police to handle it. The riot inquiry committee found reasons for widespread anti-Indian feelings in society – unregulated Indian migration, land alienation, high interest of money from the Indian *Chettyars*, competition in agriculture and industrial fields, local Buddhist women married to Indian Muslims, and conversion of women to Islam (Chakravarty, 1971). During that period of conflict, many Muslim properties, including shops, houses, and mosques, were looted, destroyed, and burned in the Burma for Burmese Only campaign. Similar anti-Muslim sentiments also erupted in Arakan. It is necessary to understand why the anti-Indian movement backlash affected Arakan Muslims.

Arakan found itself at the crossroads of two worlds – South and Southeast Asia – between Muslim-Hindu Asia and Buddhist Asia, and amidst Indo-Aryan and Mongoloid races. Throughout its history Arakan had a close relationship with Muslim Bengal in the fields of culture, economy, and politics. It is widely accepted by scholars and historians that Muslims inhabited Rakhine state hundreds of years prior to independence (EBO Briefing Paper, 2009). According to Yegar (2002, p. 23), "the Arakan region, which stretches for 350 miles along the eastern coast of the Bay of Bengal, is isolated from Burma by the Arakan Yoma, a chain of hills that are difficult to traverse". The Rohingya populated the northern part of Arakan, called the Mayu region, situated adjacent to Bengal. Arakan and Bengal have close land connections. This geographical location is separated from other parts of modern Myanmar. During the independent Arakan kingdom era (3000 BCE–18th century CE), it had more ties with the western parts of its neighbor, which is now Bangladesh. It is noted that from the 14th to 18th centuries the history of Arakan was closely linked with Muslim Bengal. Therefore, it is clear that Arakan, the western frontier state of today's Myanmar, was not part of the Burmese kingdom. The geographical position of Arakan explains the separate historical development of its Muslim population until the Burmese king Bodayapaya conquered it on December 28, 1784. The Rakhine and Rohingya ethnic leaders claimed that Arakan was colonized by the Burmans from end of 1784.[7]

The whole of Arakan consists of two major ethnic groups: Rakhine Buddhists and Rohingya Muslims. The majority is Rakhine or "Magh", who are followers of Theravada Buddhism and are ethnically close with the Burman. Wantanasombt (2013) has tried to examine how Arakanese Buddhist identities merge with the majority Burman in today's Myanmar. Wantanasombt argues that Arakan or Rakhine state was annexed as a part of Burma in 1785. During the transformation, the local people of Arakan tried to resist. Unfortunately, it was not successful. The passage of time resulted in the Arakanese Buddhists mixing with the Burmese until they assumed the same identity This was possible due to the same religious beliefs of Theravada Buddhism.

The Rohingya ethnic group was mostly Muslim and lived in the northern part of Arakan. The Muslims of Arakan-Rohingya trace their ancestry to ancient Indian people of the Chandra dynasty of Arakan, Arabs, Turks, Persians, Bengalis, and some Indo-Mongoloid people. Thus, over the centuries, the Rohingya developed from different ethnic backgrounds. It is easy to differentiate between Arakanese Muslims and other people of Myanmar. Culturally and religiously, the Rohingya Muslims are similar to the people in the southeastern part of Bangladesh. So, Clive J. Christie (1996, p. 161) noted that "in the course of the untidy evolution of modern history, many communities in these regions have found themselves 'trapped' on the 'wrong' side of the nation-state frontiers that have been created". Rohingya leaders claimed that sometimes religious issues come first and sometimes ethnic kinship issues became prominent. Muslims in Arakan were harshly affected by the Rakhine and Burmese in the 1930s because of their ethnic kinship with the Indian communities.[8] The communal violence escalated in 1942. It was the turning point, and both communities sharply divided in the name of ethnic and religious identity. Christie (1996, p. 165) argued that "one of the major effects of the war in Arakan was the development of a 'loyalty' relationship between Britain and the Arakanese Muslims. The Japanese advances into Arakan in 1942 triggered in inter-communal conflict amounting to a virtual civil war – between the Buddhist and Muslim communities".

The Government of Myanmar formed the Rakhine Inquiry Commission Report,[9] which mentioned,

> According to Rakhine accounts, at a time when the country's governing structures were non-functional due to the Second World War, Bengalis equipped with modern firearms, attacked Rakhine indigenous villages in Maungdaw and Butheetaung, killing over 20,000 Rakhine, and occupying those villages to the present day. From that time on, those areas have remained under Bengali domination.
>
> (2013, p. 8)

It should be noted here that recently produced Myanmar documents use the word "Bengali" instead of "Rohingya". In contrast, Rohingya accounts of the 1942 incident offer a different explanation.[10] Rohingya leaders have suggested that "in April 1942, armed Rakhine in connivance with Burmese nationalists carried out a program in Akyab district and massacred about 100,000 unarmed Muslims. Most of them were internally displaced, and nearly 50,000 took refuge in the British territories of Chittagong and Rangpur (currently part of northern Bangladesh)".[11] The consequences of that damage were enormous demographic changes in North Arakan. The Buddhists depopulated the Muslim population in the alluvial Kaladan and Lemro deltas. After independence, the Muslim community in Arakan immediately discovered the disadvantages of their peripheral status in a non-Muslim nation, when Muslims officials were replaced by Buddhists. As a result, tensions developed between these two groups and continues even today. The1942 massacre was the beginning of an armed struggle by these two communities to establish rights over Arakan state. Since then, the whole of Arakan has been sharply divided between Muslims and Buddhists. Neither community considers or recognizes the other's contribution to Arakan state.

Myanmar's post-independence political history suggests that the Muslim-dominated northern Arakan constituency was always dominated by the Rohingya Muslims until the 2010 election. The Rohingya Muslim minority has had a strong presence in mainstream politics since the colonial period. The parliamentary government (1948–1962) had officially declared Rohingyas one of the indigenous ethnic groups of Burma. Many researchers, historians, and journalists have elaborately discussed the role of Muslims in Burma/Myanmar's electoral process. The former Israeli diplomat and historian Moshe Yegar (1972, 2002), A. F. K. Jilani (1999), J. A. Berlie (2008), and various rights groups' documents clearly state that Rohingya Muslims have had strong political involvement in Arakan state (present Rakhine state). During the general elections for the Constituent Assembly in 1947, Sultan Ahmed and Abdul Gaffar were elected from Maungdaw and Buthidaung, respectively, and were affiliated with the Jamiat-e-Ulema, the political party of Muslims in Arakan. Sultan Ahmed was also a member of the drafting Constitution Committee of 1947 for three months, while another Muslim leader, U Rashid, was in America on an official visit (Min, 2012).

After the British colonial era, the first general election in Myanmar was held in 1951. The Rohingya Muslim-led political party Jamiat-e-Ulema got four seats in Arakan. Before the general election of 1956, the U Nu government abolished the Burma Muslim Congress and Jamiat-e-Ulema, branding them as religious parties. As a result, Muslim leaders had misapprehension about the Anti-Fascist People's Freedom League (AFPFL). The Rakhine Buddhist leaders utilized this political vacuum and took control of the AFPFL branches in Maungdaw and Buthidaung. Soon after, Muslim leaders realized the necessity of political unity with the AFPFL. The Muslim leaders Haji Abul Khair from Maungdaw South, Sultan Ahmed from

Maungdaw North, Abul Bashar from Buthidaung South, Ezhar Meah from Buthidaung North, and Abdul Gaffar were elected to the Upper House from the AFPFL in the 1956 general election (Jilani, 1999; Min, 2012).

The Rohingya Muslims demanded that North Arakan be made autonomous and subject directly to the central government in Rangoon, having no Rakhine influences (Jilani, 1999). A separate administration would also help the low standard of living of the Muslim communities and prevent abuses from the Rakhine Buddhists. On May 1, 1961, the central government created the Mayu Frontier Administration Area. It was comprised of Muslim-dominated Maungdaw, Buthidaung, and the western part of Rathidaung townships. It was under the Ministry of Defense and was controlled from Rangoon. A special police force known as Mayu Ray was formed, and members were recruited from local Muslims; so the law and order situation improved (Jilani, 1999, p. 8). The total population of May Yu Frontier Area is nearly half a million. Most people in the area are engaged in agriculture and fisheries. The majority of the people are Rohingya, and the rest of the groups are Rakhine, Dai Nat, Myo, and Khmee (Yegar, 2002). The headquarters of the May Yu Frontier Area was in the border town of Maungdaw. The Rohingya Muslims dominated the May Yu Frontier region, which was controlled by the central government before 1964.

Arakan historian Jacques P. Leider interpreted it differently: "Prime Minister U Nu's government in the 1950s earned support from the Muslims and political reward them in the early 1960s when the short-lived 'Mayu Frontier Administration' in North Arakan was created" (Leider, 2017). Volume 9 of the Myanmar Encyclopedia (1964, pp. 89–90) discusses in detail the Rohingyas populating the May Yu Frontier Area. The Yangon-based Rohingya political leaders claimed that it was the only administration that favored Rohingyas during the post-independence history in Burma. The Burma Broadcasting Services aired twice a week in the Rohingya language until October 24, 1965 (Nyein, 1976). This evidence shows that Rohingya language broadcasts stopped after the military coup in the 1960s. The Rohingya leaders' statements and other documents suggest that a policy of exclusion of Rohingya started after General Ne Win took over state power. During the parliamentary era, the Rohingyas enjoyed and actively participated in all government activities.

Regardless of political differences, the Rohingya Muslims had representation in *Hlauttaw* (parliament) under the Ne Win socialist regime. From 1988 to 1997, the military government was known as the State Law and Order Restoration Council (SLORC), which replaced the Burma Socialist Program Party (BSPP). The new military government conducted general elections in May 1990. It was the first multiparty election since 1960, after which the country had been ruled by military dictators.

A future for the Rohingya in Myanmar 65

During that general election, associate and naturalized citizens were permitted to vote but not allowed to contest the election. The Union Election Commission allowed the Rohingyas the right to vote and contest the general election. In fact, the Rohingyas were permitted to form political parties in 1989. Two parties were formed: the Students and Youth League for Mayu Development and the National Democratic Party for Human Rights (NDPH). The titles behind the names as well as the biographies of the NDPH's four nominated MPs show that most of them had received a university degree in Burma or Myanmar and had been in government service.

The Rohingyas again were allowed the right to vote in the 2008 referendum. Before the 2010 elections, two new political parties were formed to represent the interests of the Muslims of Rakhine state, the National Democratic Party for Development (NDPD) and the Democracy and Human Rights Party (DHRP). In the 2010 elections, two Rohingya candidates were victorious from Muslim-dominated areas under the banner of NDPD. Later, the Union Election Commission invalidated their candidacies.[12] As a result, the runners–up, supported by the military, that is, the Union Solidarity and Development Party (USDP) candidates, became MPs from those constituencies. These legislators were from the Rohingya Muslim community and played active roles in the House of Representatives (Pyithu Hluttaw) from

Photo 3.3 Rohingya gathering after Friday prayer in Bangkok, Thailand

2010 to 2015. Shwe Maung (alias Abdul Razak) was elected in 2010 as a member of the ruling USDP and later announced his candidacy in the 2015 election as an independent. He was one of the few voices in parliament to speak on behalf of the Rohingya as a stateless Muslim minority residing in Rakhine state. Despite Shwe Maung's position as a parliamentarian, the Election Commission reportedly turned him down on the grounds that his parents were not Burmese citizens, a claim that he maintained was untrue (Mann, 2015). This author conducted an interview with Shwe Maung, MP from the USDP, at his residence in Yangon in 2013. He stated that his late father, Abdul Hadi, was a reserve member of the ruling BSPP central committee in the 1970s. Above all, these discussions and officials' documents are a testament to the long and continuous involvement of Rohingyas in Myanmar's political process.

Rohingya exclusion

Despite the Rohingya's political presence in Myanmar, large numbers of that community were arbitrarily deprived of their citizenship under the 1982 Citizenship Law. The military regime of Burma branded the Muslims as resident foreigners and effectively reduced them to the status of stateless (Ahmed, 2010). According to Berlie (2008), the identity of the Rohingya or Muslims of Arakan in Burma was quite different from Muslims of South Asian or Indian origin. However, the Government of Myanmar has consistently claimed that this minority Muslim group migrated during colonial times. Earlier it was mentioned that before the 1962 military coup, the ethnic Muslim minority Rohingya did not face a citizenship question under the state framework. Under the 1947 Constitution and the 1948 Burma Citizenship Act, the Rohingya enjoyed full citizenship rights. General Ne Win's government made a list of national ethnicities in 1972 to conduct the census. That was the first time the military government treated them as "Chittagongian–Rakhine" (Haque, 2014). According to that identity, these people were Bangladeshi settlers in Arakan state. It can be said that General Ne Win had a long-term plan to eradicate the Rohingya's identity in Burma. General Ne Win also changed the ancient name Arakan and called it Rakhine state. From that time, the Rohingya were deprived of their original identity under the Union of Burma. In 1978, the military government conducted Operation Nagamin[13] to identify illegal Bangladeshi settlers in Arakan. Consequent to this operation, thousands of Rohingya became refugees in neighboring Bangladesh. Within a year, Rohingyas had repatriated to Burma. Finally, General Ne Win's government passed the 1982 Citizenship Law, after which Rohingya Muslims became *de jure* stateless in their ancestors' homeland.

This law is fully discriminatory, and Rohingya are now unwanted people in Myanmar. The whole concept of citizenship in Myanmar is relatively more complicated than in other countries. In Myanmar, citizenship is based on ethnic identity, and the government recognizes 135 ethnicities in the country under the 1982 Citizenship Law, not including the Rohingya. The 1982 Citizenship Law also recognizes "a person who is already a citizen on the date this Law comes into force is a citizen. Action, however shall be taken under section 18 for infringement of the provision of that section" (section 6). It means whoever once enjoyed citizenship will be automatically citizens. Therefore, Rohingya meet the criteria of section 6 and should be treated as citizens of the Union of Burma. But, section 3 specifically mentions the ethnic name, where the Rohingya was excluded from the list (Haque, 2017a. p.458). As a result, the Indo-Aryan race Rohingya were arbitrarily deprived of their nationality in the name of pure blood or so-called indigenous ethnicity. The whole law is self-contradictory and intends to exclude the Rohingya.

The Government of Myanmar claimed that Rohingyas are not listed among the 135 ethnic groups, so they are not eligible for full citizenship (Kipgen, 2019). But historical facts and figures do not support the government's arguments on the criteria of so-called indigenous ethnicity. After communal riots in 2012, anti-Rohingya propaganda is still going on, and it is highly projected in the media. Frequently, the regime launches drive operations, creates communal riots, and makes forced relocations to sweep out the Muslim population.

Hatred against the Rohingya

It is important that during the colonial period and in the aftermath of independence, the Rohingya identity was shaped in different forms. Sometimes, they were treated more like those with migrated South Asian origin in Myanmar. Sometimes their religious identity came to the forefront to have them treated as a minority. Strategically, it is easier for the Myanmar Buddhist regime to label the Rohingya as part of global terrorism. The ruling elites' attitudes against the Rohingya community are related to their religion. The recently formed 969 widely campaigned and distributed anti-Islam flyers among the Buddhist communities inside the country.[14] This campaign indicates communal instigation against the Muslims.

There is another strong misconception about Muslim population growth being a real threat to national integrity in Buddhist-dominated Myanmar. This perception has been strong since the 1930s. According to formal and informal discussion with Muslim leaders, most of the Buddhists often claim that Islam is a religion that swallowed Hinduism and Buddhism in

Indonesia, Malaysia, and the whole Indian peninsula. Some researchers argue that "discrimination against the Rohingya has been credited to not only the ambiguity of their origin, but also because they are Muslims in a Buddhist country. The legitimate unifiers of Burma have been the Burmans (major ethnic group), and these unifiers have always been Buddhist" (Fajri, 2010, p. 7). For that reason, ruling elites including the military and monks have drawn closer in Myanmar to resist the Muslims and use Islamophobia against the Rohingya.

The Rohingya became isolated from other ethnic groups because of their different ethnic identity. This is deeply rooted in Myanmar society as a cultural problem. According to the Rakhine Commission Report, "the public generally view the Bengalis as being merciless, selfish and unsavory" (2013, p. 18). This societal perception was developed against the Rohingya in the name of racism. The words "merciless", "selfish", and "unsavory" indicate the intensity of racism in Arakan. The whole state machinery instigates a hatred strategy against the Rohingya presence. Even the media and civic groups are against them (Rakhine Commission Report, 2013). All try to justify their stance in the name of racial purity.

It is a reality at this moment that the word "Rohingya" is taboo in the former capital city of Rangoon, and it is one of the banned names by Myanmar officials. The National Museum in Yangon, which has a collection of materials of all sub-nationalities (labeled by the government as "national races" and categorized into seven groups in terms of language origin – Shan, Mon, Karen, Kayah, Chin, Kachin, and Rakhine), makes no mention of the Rohingyas, nor does it have any collection dedicated to them (Ahmed, 2010). In the name of racial purity, Rohingya do not fit into Myanmar. This argument became more popular and strong after the 2012 communal violence.

It can be assumed that the whole society has become hostile to the Rohingya. In Myanmar, most people strongly believe that the brown complexion of the Rohingya is not consistent with the Myanmar state ethnic identity. It is persistent in Myanmar society that "Rohingya do not look like us, and there is no place for Rohingya in Myanmar".[15] Rakhine scholars and politicians often claim that there is no Rohingya ethnic group in Burma and the term "Rohingya" is a Bengali word.[16] The underlying cause of these allegations against the Rohingya is their different ethnicity. Rohingya leader Habibur Rahman stated that systematic propaganda and vilification have been carried out against the Rohingya and other Muslims with the slogan "Arakan is for Rakhine". Those who oppose the presence of the Rohingya espouse the idea that Rakhine and Buddhism are synonymous terms, and Muslims have no place in Arakan and should be kicked out.[17] This argument is also supported by the Fortify Rights report, which found that "many Rakhine have been intent on forcing Rohingya out of what they regard as

Photo 3.4 Displaced Rohingya shelter in Cox's Bazar, Bangladesh

their exclusive ancestral homeland" (2014, p. 9). There is no significant difference of opinion between the NLD government and main opposition party USDP about Rohingya ethnicity, race, and identity.

Rohingya's struggle for existence in Myanmar

Earlier it was mentioned that the whole of Myanmar society perceives the Rohingya as being outsiders and a threat to national integrity. Even the media and civic groups fail to take a stand against genocide and other atrocities. Generically it can be said that large numbers of Rohingya are now living outside of the country as refugees, asylum seekers, migrant workers, or immigrants. Numerous community organizations were established to support the Rohingya after the 2012 communal riots in Myanmar, but historically few Rohingya political organizations have been active since the 1970s, although Yangon-based Rohingya political parties did play a vital role in establishing their rights, and they firmly believe that the Rohingya issue should be resolved within the Myanmar state framework. They denied any involvement with separatist-militant groups, preferring to live in peaceful political coexistence in Myanmar. The overall situation for Rohingyas is difficult because the state, through the *Tatmadaw*,[18] conducted clearance operations and atrocities widely described as acts of genocide.

The Rohingya issue is now focused in two major areas: recognizing identity and ensuring a peaceful life in the home of their ancestors. It should be mentioned here that refugee repatriation is linked with the citizenship issue.

Since the military operations against them, more than 1 million Rohingya have fled the country because of well-founded fears of persecution. Sources have witnessed that thousands of people have been killed, including children, women, and old men. After two years, forcibly displaced people have not been able return to their homes. Moreover, 128,000 Rohingya and other displaced Muslims are still living in crowded camps in Rakhine state six years after Buddhist mobs razed most of their homes (Aung & Lewis, 2018).

The newly formed Rohingya National Forum comprises Rohingya organizations, individuals from inside Myanmar, and the global diaspora. After three days of consultation in Kuala Lumpur in March 2019, they agreed on a number of resolutions for the greater interest of their community. The Rohingya National Forum reaffirmed that Rohingyas are an indigenous people with roots back to the ancient kingdom of Arakan (Rakhine), and they wish to live in peace and harmony, with dignity and the same rights as the other ethnic groups of Myanmar. This forum also sought solidarity with other ethnic groups in and from Myanmar (Rohingya National Forum, 2019).

The Yangon-based Rohingya leader Abu Tahay explained that Rohingyas are struggling to gain full citizenship in accordance with the Aung San-Atlee Agreement signed on January 27, 1947, and the Nu-Atlee Agreement of October 1 of the same year, as defined in Article 11, subclauses a, b, and c, of the 1947 Constitution. But later, the military government arbitrarily refused to adhere to the agreed terms and promulgated the 1982 Citizenship Law based on race identity (email conversation, June 2019). This became the pivotal point of this whole crisis. To ensure a fair and sustainable solution, Kyaw Min, alias Shamsul Anwar, chair of the Democracy and Human Rights Party, tried to clarify their stand, arguing that Rohingya representatives should be included in the refugee repatriation process. He explained that the whole displacement issue is not between Myanmar and Bangladesh but rather was rooted in relations between the Rohingya community and the Government of Myanmar. As a community leader, he was also seeking assistance from Bangladesh and the UN (email conversation, June 2019). The Government of Myanmar's explanation that the Rohingyas' forced displacement is a consequence of the violent conflict inside Rakhine state is not borne out by historical evidence, so he has called on all stakeholders to reject such an explanation and work earnestly to resolve the long-standing Rohingya citizenship issue in Myanmar. The 88 Generation Rohingya Muslim activist Ko Ko Linn, alias Mohammad Kalim,[19] agrees that full citizenship rights for Rohingya must be restored with constitutional guarantees. Furthermore, Nurul Islam, the UK-based exiled Rohingya leader and chair of the Arakan Rohingya National Organization (ARNO), fully supports the inside leaders' demand that Rohingya citizenship be restored to ensure their collective rights as people of Arakan. He also accuses the Government of

Myanmar of delaying refugee repatriation. During our conversation, Nurul[20] reminded that "it was a historical blinder that Rohingya were repatriated as 'residents' of Burma and the term 'citizens' was not mentioned in the repatriation agreement of 1978 signed between Bangladesh and Burma". However, he firmly believes that this time displaced Rohingya from inside and outside of the country will return to their homes in Rakhine state and rebuild their lives in peaceful coexistence with all other ethnic groups and religious communities in Myanmar. Currently, refugee repatriation is one of the major agenda items for the international community in addressing the Rohingya issue. It is rather frustrating for the Myanmar side, and the government is creating numerous obstacles against repatriation.

"The Myanmar government is ready to grant all those who come back with a certificate of residence while those who are eligible can apply for citizenship", stated U Kyaw Tint Swe,, minister for the Office of the State Counselor during the 25th International Conference on the Future of Asia in Tokyo on May 31, 2019 (cited in Kumar, 2019). He also mentioned that Bangladesh has not honored a bilateral arrangement inked in November 2017 meant to facilitate the repatriation of displaced people and other minorities who fled violence in the state of Rakhine. It is a controversial statement that literally creates barriers for repatriation of refugees. The Rohingya leader Kyaw Min, alias Shamsul Anwar, is suspicious of the Government of Myanmar's approach. "If Myanmar is ready to accept all refugees, it will be highly praised. But the Myanmar government has already rejected six thousand refugees out of eight thousand on a list provided by the Bangladesh authorities" (email conversation, June 2019). The minister's second point is a real reflection of the injustice the Government of Myanmar has been continuously pursuing and practicing against the Muslims of Arakan.

The Rohingya people have held the National Registration Card (NRC) since the time of independence. They enjoyed the right to vote and to be elected or to contest all national elections in Myanmar up to the 2010 election. Basically, the Government of Myanmar is not sincere and imposes barriers against their peaceful return. Kyaw Min, alias Shamsul Anwar, is worried that repatriation of 300 refugees per day will take more than a decade to complete (email conversation, June 2019). Seemingly, the UN agencies concerned have no role in the repatriation process except for providing technical support. It is not a practical solution. Moreover, returnees do not know where within Myanmar they are going. The first batch of Rohingyas was scheduled to return mid-November 2018, but it did not happen amid unwillingness of the Rohingyas due to the lack of a congenial environment in Rakhine state. After nearly one year, the ten-member delegation, led by Myint Thu (the permanent secretary of the Myanmar Foreign Ministry), had a meeting with Rohingya Muslims at refugee camps. Myanmar officials' meetings over two days with Rohingya leaders failed to make any consensus on the issue of repatriation. Mohibullah, chair of the Arakan Rohingya Society for Peace and Human Rights, who led a 30-member team in the meeting, stated that the Myanmar delegation had come with the same old proposals that they had rejected before. He also mentioned that "not a single Rohingya would return to Myanmar if they were not guaranteed citizenship" (cited in *The Daily Star*, 2019).

Despite all these limitations, the Rohingya leadership inside Myanmar remains hopeful that a long-lasting peace can be arranged for their community. They would like to cooperate with the government and other political forces to advance a positive peace. Abu Tahay believes that a positive peace can be achieved and sustained by providing a taxonomy that breaks down into eight distinct but independent pillars (email conversation, June 2019): (1) well-functioning government; (2) equitable distribution of resources; (3) free flow of information; (4) good relationships with neighbors; (5) high-level human capital; (6) acceptance of the rights of others; (7) low level of corruption; and (8) sound business development. Simultaneously, all parties should avoid any kind of violence and conflict, including racism and chauvinistic attitudes. Exiled Rohingya leader Ko Ko Linn, alias Mohammad Kalim, stated that if the Government of Myanmar and Rakhine Buddhists do not agree to take them back and continue their hard-line attitude, then the international community should intervene. If the international community is reluctant to deal with this matter due to geopolitical interests, then the Rohingya have the right to take responsibility for their own safety and protection. But, he still believes that although the Rohingya have been victims of genocide, they can safely return to their homes.[21] The diaspora, including some Rohingya leaders inside Myanmar, have proposed another viable option to solve this long-standing crisis. It is at an elementary stage, and views are still being exchanged, but basically, they are seeking a solution under Chapter XI: Article 73, Declaration Regarding Non-Self-Governing Territories of the UN Charter (1945), namely, the following points:

a to ensure, with due respect for the culture of the peoples concerned, their political, economic, social, and educational advancement, their just treatment, and their protection against abuses;
b to develop self-government, to take due account of the political aspirations of the peoples, and to assist them in the progressive development of their free political institutions, according to the particular circumstances of each territory and its peoples and their varying stages of advancement; and,
c to further international peace and security.

Nurul Islam, one of the seniormost Rohingya leaders, stated that through the UN Charter a safe zone can be established for the Rohingya in Rakhine state that should be monitored by the international community. But he cautions that they do not want to have the same bad experience as victims in former Yugoslavia or Rwanda (email conversation, June 2019). After nearly three years of mass destruction, the UNSC failed to take effective measures against the perpetrators, and no visible initiatives have been proposed to ensure the lives of the Rohingyas and their safe return to their homes. It has been argued here that the issue of restoring the Rohingyas' citizenship is more important, but a satisfactory response from community and government is far away. There is another major security threat in Rakhine state: regular fighting between the Myanmar military and the Rakhine ultranationalist-supported Arakan Army (AA). Establishing a peaceful coexistence among the ethnic groups in Rakhine has become more complicated after the violent exchanges between the Myanmar military and the AA in Rakhine state. During exchanges of gunfire, innocent Rohingyas are frequently killed. There is no justice for these victims. It should also be mentioned that the AA is struggling to establish a right to self-determination in their ancestors' land.

Conclusion

It is an established perception in Myanmar society that Rohingya Muslims are illegal migrants and a threat to national security. For that reason, after the first Rohingya influx in 1978, the Government of Myanmar made a new citizenship law to exclude the Rohingya Muslims in the name of so-called indigenous race. In modern nation-states, the majority commonly accuses the minority of lack of loyalty to the state. It is, therefore, not exceptional in the case of Rohingya Muslims that after military intervention in Myanmar history, not only for Rohingya but also other ethnic minorities, they are treated as anti-state elements. In the name of national interest, the Burman-dominated military regime tried to establish that especially Rohingyas are a threat to national integrity.

A number of interviewees in this study think that the whole state machinery failed to accommodate national minorities in mainstream politics. Specifically, the Rohingyas' ethnic-religious identity was not only rejected, but they have been also persecuted by state and nonstate actors in Myanmar. The ongoing violence in Rakhine state and the government's unwillingness to intervene proves that Rohingyas are in the same situation as before democratization in Myanmar. It is clear that the Aung San Suu Kyi-led elected government has failed to take any measures to protect the Rohingya from the Myanmar military's so-called clearing operations.

Despite international community pressure, the Government of Myanmar makes barriers to Rohingya refugees safely returning to their homes. In that context, the Rohingya community at home and abroad strongly suggests that refugee repatriation is not the solution to this whole crisis. There are a few issues that should be resolved before refugees return; a safe zone can be established in the northern part of Rakhine state under UN supervision, citizenship can be restored in the present Myanmar nation-state framework, and the collective rights of Rohingyas can be assured.

The UN and other international bodies have often condemned the Government of Myanmar's and Rakhine state's governments' attitudes toward the Rohingya. Yet, this has had no effect on the Rohingya's identity and their life in Myanmar. Because of a lack of human rights enforcement mechanisms, Rohingya suffering has not ended but, rather, expands every day. It can be concluded that perpetrators should not go unpunished in the case of Rohingya in Myanmar, and no atrocities are justifiable in the name of national integrity.

Notes

1 The word "kala" derives from the Pali word meaning "noble"; it also means "black" in Bengali and other languages. The term is associated with racist connotations in the Burmese language and is often used to refer to outsiders from the subcontinent, including Bangladeshis, Indians, Nepalis, Sri Lankans, and Pakistanis. To Rohingya, being called "kala" is to deny their historical connection to Rakhine state.
2 Formal and informal conversation in different times at Yangon in July 2012, July 2013, March 2014, and May 2017 and Thailand in 2014 and 2018.
3 The Burmese Way to Socialism is an economic treatise written in April 1962 by the Revolutionary Council, shortly after the coup, as a blueprint for economic development, reducing foreign influence in Burma and increasing the role of the military. This doctrine has been described as anti-Western, neutralist, and socialist in nature, characterized also by an extensive dependence on the military and emphasis on the rural populace, specifically to ensure the Burman ethnic dominance in state power.
4 Interview with the leaders of Rohingya Solidarity Organizations (RSO), April 2014 in Cox's Bazar and February 2017, in Chittagong, Bangladesh.
5 Interview with Hossain Kader, May 2017, in Yangon.
6 The *Chettiars* are a subgroup of the Tamil community originating from *Chettinad* in Tamil Nadu, India. Historically, the *Chettiars* are most commonly associated with the moneylending profession. In Myanmar political history, few groups have been as vilified as the *Chettiars*. A community of Indian moneylenders, the *Chettiars* were crucial agents in transforming Burma into the rice bowl of Asia. Following the global depression of the 1930s, Burmese agriculture became severely distressed and wide-scale loan default saw the transfer of much of Burma's cultivatable land to the *Chettiars*, who were demonized and made scapegoats for the vices of colonialism.

7 Interview with Rohingya and Rakhine leaders in Chiang Mai and Mae Sot, March 2019.
8 Interview with Abu Tahay, chair, UNDP, May 2014, in Yangon, and Nurul Islam, chair of ARNO, February 2017, in Chittagong.
9 The Rakhine Inquiry Commission was established on August, 17, 2012, under the authority of the president's executive order to discover the root causes of communal violence, provide recommendations to prevent the recurrence of violence in the future, and promote peaceful coexistence.
10 Interview with different Rohingya political groups inside Myanmar in 2014 and diaspora Rohingya leaders in Bangkok in 2013 and 2019 and Kuala Lumpur in 2019.
11 Interview with different Rohingya political groups inside Myanmar in 2014 and diaspora Rohingya leaders in Bangkok in 2013 and 2019 and Kuala Lumpur in 2019.
12 Interview with Abu Tahay, chair, UNDP, May 2014, in Yangon.
13 The Burmese immigration and military authorities conducted Operation Nagamin, a national effort to register citizens and screen out foreigners prior to a national census. The operation began on February 6, 1978. In the span of three months, approximately 200,000 to 250,000 Rohingya Muslims fled to Bangladesh. The Government of Burma estimated that 150,000 fled during the operation and proclaimed that the mass exodus signified that Rohingyas were in fact "illegal immigrants". On July 31, 1978, the governments of Burma and Bangladesh reached an agreement regarding the repatriation of Rohingya refugees and they returned to Burma following the agreement.
14 Interview with Wali Ullah, secretary general, NDPD, May 2017, in Yangon.
15 Interview, anonymous Myanmar civil society members, March 2014 and May 2017, in Yangon.
16 During the informal discussion and interview with Rakhine scholars and activists, March 2014 and May 2017, in Yangon and February 2018 in Chiang Mai, Thailand.
17 Interview with Habibur Rahman, vice chairman, ARNO, November 2013 and November 2018, in Chittagong.
18 The *Tatmadaw* is the official name of the armed forces of Myanmar. It is administered by the Ministry of Defense and composed of the army, navy, and air force.
19 Interview with 88 Generation activist and Rohingya leader Ko Ko Linn, alias Mohammad Kalim, Chittagong, June 2019.
20 Interview with Nurul Islam, chair, ARNO, April 2019, in Kuala Lumpur.
21 Interview with 88 Generation activist and Rohingya leader Ko Ko Linn, alias Mohammad Kalim, in Chittagong, June 2019.

References

Aljazeera. (2012). *The Rohingya: A humanitarian crisis*. Retrieved from www.aljazeera.com/programmes/insidestory/2012/08/201281542835204365.html

Ahmed, I. (Ed.). (2010). *The plight of the stateless Rohingyas: Response of the state, society & the international community*. Dhaka: University Press Limited.

Andersen, M., & Taylor, F. (2006). *Sociology: Understanding a diverse society*. Belmont: Thomson Corporation.

Aung, T. T., & Lewis, S. (2018). *"We can't go anywhere" – Myanmar closes Rohingya camps but entrenches segregation*. Retrieved from www.thestar.com.my/news/world/2018/12/06/we-cant-go-anywhere–Myanmar-closes-Rohingya-camps–but-entrenches-segregation/

Berlie, J. A. (2008). *The Burmanization of Myanmar's Muslims*. Bangkok: White Lotus Press.

Brown, D. (2007). Ethnic conflict and civil nationalism. A model. In J. L. Peackok, P. M. Thorntorn, & P. B. Inman (Eds.), *Identity matters: Ethnic and sectarian conflict* (Ch. 1). New York: Berghahn Books.

Chakravarty, N. R. (1971). *The Indian minority in Burma*. Oxford: Oxford University Press.

Charter of the United Nations. (1945). *Chapter XI: Declaration regarding non-self-governing territories*. Retrieved from www.un.org/en/sections/un-charter/chapter-xi/index.html

Christie, C. J. (1996). *A modern history of southeast Asia: Decolonization, nationalism and separatism*. London: I.B. Tauris Publishers.

The Daily Star. (2019). *Myanmar to consider Rohingyas as foreigners*. Retrieved from www.thedailystar.net/backpage/news/myanmar-consider-rohingyas-foreigners-1778449

Daniyal, S. (2017). *Forgotten history: Like the Rohingya, Indians too were once driven out of Myanmar*. Retrieved from www.dhakatribune.com/world/south-asia/2017/09/12/forgotten-history-like-rohingya-indians-driven-myanmar

EBO Briefing Paper. (2009). *The Rohingyas: Bengali Muslims or Arakan Rohingyas?* Briefing Paper No. 2, 1–5. Retrieved from www.burmalibrary.org/docs6/EBO_Briefing_Paper_No._2_-_The_Rohingyas.pdf

Fajri, A. (2010). *In the absence of citizenship: Policies and actions of neighboring states the course of Rohingya refugees in Indonesia*. Thailand and Bangladesh, MA: University of San Diego.

Fortify Rights. (2014). *Policies of persecution: Ending abusive state policies against Rohingya Muslims in Myanmar*. Retrieved from www.fortifyrights.org/downloads/Policies_of_Persecution_Feb_25_Fortify_Rights.pdf

Haque, M. M. (2014). *Rights of non-citizens and concern for security: The case of Rohingya in Burma and Bangladesh* (Ph. D), Mahidol University.

Haque, M. M. (2017a, November). Rohingya ethnic Muslim minority and the 1982 citizenship law in Burma. *Journal of Muslim Minority Affairs*, 37 (4), pp. 454–469. Retrieved from www.tandfonline.com/doi/full/10.1080/13602004.2017.1399600

Haque, M. M. (2017b, December). Political transition in Burma/Myanmar: Status of Rohingya and other Muslim minorities. *South Asian Journal of Policy and Governance (SJPG), 41*(2), ISSN 2091-0207.

Head, J. (2017). *Rohingya crisis: Finding out the truth about ARSA militants*. Retrieved from www.bbc.com/news/world-asia-41521268

Jilani, A. F. K. (1999). *The Rohingyas of Arakan: Their Quest for Justice* (1st ed.), Chittagong: Taj Library.

Kipgen, N. (2019). The Rohingya crisis: The centrality of identity and citizenship. *Journal of Muslim Minority Affairs, 39*(1), 61–74. Retrieved from www.tandfonline.com/doi/full/10.1080/13602004.2019.1575019

Kumar, P. (2019). *Myanmar says Bangladesh not helping refugee return*. Retrieved from https://asia.nikkei.com/Spotlight/The-Future-of-Asia-2019/Myanmar-Says-Bangladesh-not-helping-refugee-return

Kuper, L. (Ed.). (1974). *Race, science and society*. London: George Allen & Unwin Ltd.

Lederer, E. M. (2018). *UN investigator: Genocide still taking place in Myanmar*. Retrieved from www.apnews.com/bb92e8db60444caeba4787d42c9280e0.

Leider, J. P. (2017). *Interview on the frictions in the Rakhine state are less about islamophobia than Rohingya-Phobia*. Retrieved from https://thewire.in/external-affairs/frictions-rakhine-state-less-islamophobia-rohingya-phobia.

Mann, Z. (2015). *Rohingya MP and Mandalay Doctor Barred from contesting November election*. Retrieved from www.irrawaddy.com/news/burma/rohingya-mp-and-mandalay-doctor-barred-from-contesting-november-election.html

Min, K. (2012). *An assessment of the question of Rohingyas' nationality: Legal nexus between Rohingya and the state*. Chittagong: Arakan Historical Society.

Mullins, J., & Aye, M. M. (2014). *Panthay Muslims protect their name*. Retrieved from www.mmtimes.com/national-news/mandalay-upper-myanmar/9998-panthay-muslims-protect-their-name.html

Musaji, S. (2016). *Islamophobia: Real or Imagined*. Retrieved from http://www.theamericanmuslim.org/tam.php/features/articles/islamophobia_real_or_imagined/0016131

The Rakhine Inquiry Commission. (2013). *Final Report of Inquiry Commission on Sectarian Violence in Rakhine State*. Retrieved from www.burmalibrary.org/docs15/Rakhine_Commission_Reporten-red.pdf

The Union of Burma/Myanmar Official Encyclopedia (Burmese language). (1964), Vol. 9, pp. 89–90, Rangoon: The Government Printing House.

Nyein, K. (1976). *30 Years of Myanmar Radio [manuscript] Paya Road*. Rangoon, Burma: New Broadcasting Building.

Office of the High Commissioner for Human Rights. (1965). *International convention on the elimination of all forms of racial discrimination*. Retrieved from www.ohchr.org/en/professionalinterest/pages/cerd.aspx.

Omi, M., & Winant, H. (1994). *Racial formations* (2nd ed.). New York: Routledge.

Petersen, H. E. (2019). *Myanmar police hunt 'Buddhist bin Laden' over Suu Kyi comments*. Retrieved from www.theguardian.com/world/2019/may/29/myanmar-police-hunt-buddhist-bin-laden-over-suu-kyi-comments

Popham, P. (2013). *Buddhist Bin Laden' Wirathu unharmed by car bomb attack in Burma*. Retrieved from www.independent.co.uk/news/world/asia/buddhist-bin-laden-wirathu-unharmed-by-car-bomb-attack-in-burma-8727008.html

Rohingya National Forum. (2019). Unpublished press release, Kuala Lumpur.

Taylor, R. H. (2007). British policy towards Myanmar and the creation of the Burma problem. In N. Ganesan & K. H. Hlaing (Eds.), *Myanmar: State, society and ethnicity*. Singapore: Institute of Southeast Asian Studies.

Volkan, V. (2008). *Large group identity, international relations and psychoanalysis*. Presented Deutsche Psychoanalytische Gesellschaft e.V. (DGP) Meeting Gasteig Cultural Center, Rosenheimer Platz.

Wantanasombt, A. (2013). *The Rohingya from Burma perspective*. MA. Bangkok: Chulalongkorn University.

William, M. (1993). Burmese hell. *World Policy Journal* (The MIT Press and the World Policy Institute), *10*(2), 47–56. JSTOR 40209305.

Yegar, M. (1972). *The Muslims of Burma: A study of a minority group.* Wiesbaden: Otto Harrassowitz.

Yegar, M. (2002). *Between integration and secession: The Muslim communities of the southern Philippines, Southern Thailand and Western Burma/Myanmar.* Lanham and New York: Lexington Books.

Index

Note: Page numbers in *italic* indicate a figure on the corresponding page.

25th International Conference on the Future of Asia (2019) 71
88 Generation Rohingya Muslim 70
969 movement *see* anti-Rohingya Muslim campaign

Act East policy 46
Ahmed, Sultan 63
Allied Powers 21
Al-Qaeda 58
AlTamimi, Yussef 6
Anan Commission Report 48
Anglo-Burma Wars 60
Anti-Fascist People's Freedom League (AFPFL) 63
anti-Indian movement 61
anti-Islamic propaganda 58, 59
anti-Muslim sentiments 61
anti-Rohingya Muslim campaign 58–59
anti-Rohingya propaganda 67
Anwar, Shamsul *see* Kyaw Min
Aqa Mul Mujahidin 4, 16, 20, 58
Arakan *see* Rakhine state
Arakan Army (AA) 73
Arakan Rohingya National Organization (ARNO) 70
Arakan Rohingya Salvation Army (ARSA) *see Aqa Mul Mujahidin*
Arakan Rohingya Society for Peace and Human Rights 72
Arakan Rohingya Union 14
Arendt, Hannah 24, 25
ARSO 24
Asian Highway 39

Association of Southeast Asian Nations (ASEAN) 34, 36, 40; in Rohingya crisis 44–45
Aung San-Atlee Agreement (1947) 70
Aung San Suu Kyi 43, 59, 73

Ba Maw 61
Bangladesh 4, 11, 15, 19, 26n1, 45, 47, 48, 61, 71; demand for natural gas 37–38; policy conundrum for 45–47; refugee problem in 19, 38, 45–46, 48; Rohingya's migration to 16, 19, 20, 34; *see also* Government of Bangladesh
Bangladesh, China, India, Myanmar (BCIM) Corridor 39
Bangladesh–Myanmar bilateral relationship 37–39
Bashar, Abul 64
Bay of Bengal Initiative for Multi-Sectoral Technical and Economic Cooperation (BIMSTEC) 39
Belt and Road Initiative (BRI) 36–37, 43, 44, 46
Berlie, J. A. 63
Berryman, John 35
bilateral agreements 4, 5, 20
bilateral international relations 8
bodhisattva 10
Bodu Bala Sena 9
Brassard, Francis 9–10
Brazil, Russia, China, India, and South Africa (BRICS) 35
Britain 60

British India Company 60
Brzezinski, Zbigniew 35
Buddhism 6, 8–9, 25, 58, 67, 68; fundamental aspects of 11
Buddhist-Muslim riots (2012) 53, 58, 67–69
Buddhist Power Force (BBS) *see* Bodu Bala Sena
Buddhists 2–4, 6, 10, 63, 67; Arakanese/Rakhine 7, 9, 15, 53, 61, 62, 64, 72; armed groups 5; monastic violence 10; monks 10, 53; society 8; tensions between Muslims and 63; theory and practice 9
Burma *see* Myanmar
Burma Broadcasting Services 64
Burma Citizenship Act (1948) 66
Burma Citizenship Law *see* Pyithu Hluttaw Law No. 4 (1982)
Burma Muslim Congress 63
Burma Socialist Program Party (BSPP) 64, 66
Burmese Way to Socialism 56–57, 74n3
Buthidaung 63, 64

Cambodia 45
Cambodia, Laos, Myanmar and Vietnam (CLMV) 40
Camus, Albert 24, 25
Canadian Friends of Burma Public Conference (2002) 27n16
Chakravarty, Nalini Ranjan 60
Charter of the Nuremberg Tribunal 21, 22
Chettiars 60, 61, 74n6
China 34–37, 41, 42, 46, 47
China–Myanmar bilateral relationship 36, 37, 42–44
China–Myanmar Economic Corridor (CMEC) 37, 43
China–Myanmar oil pipeline 43
China National Petroleum Corporation 43
Chittagongian settlements 53
Christie, Clive J. 62
Chulia Muslim 59
citizenship 4, 5, 7, 10, 13, 15, 39, 45, 48, 52, 54, 55, 57, 59, 66, 67, 69, 73
civilian authorities 18

civilian courts 18
civil rights 22, 25
clearance operations 16, 24, 73
colonialism 22, 39
commerce 35, 39
communitarianism 1
compassion 8, 10
Constitution Committee: 1947 63, 66, 70; 1948 13
Convention on the Non-Applicability of Statutory Limitations to War Crimes and Crimes Against Humanity (1968) 22; Article II 23
Convention Relating to the Status of Refugees (1951) 45
Council of Foreign Relations (2019) 36
counterinsurgency 4, 5, 8, 41
Cox Bazar region 45
crimes 5, 45; atrocity 4, 16–19; against humanity 5, 16–19, 21–25
criminality 25
culture 55; Islamic 58

Daily Star 40
Dalai Lama 11
Davis, Anthony 58
Declaration of the Rights of Persons Belonging to National or Ethnic, Religious and Linguistic Minorities (1992) 28n45
Declaration on the Inadmissibility of Intervention in the Domestic Affairs of the States and the Protection of Their Independence and Sovereignty 22–23
Declaration Regarding Non-Self-Governing Territories of the UN Charter (1945): Chapter XI: Article 73 72, 73
dehumanization 57
democracy 7, 44; movement 40; transition 20
Democracy and Human Rights Party (DHRP) 65, 70
demographic transition 4, 8–10
demonization 57
Derrida, Jacques 24
Dhaka Tribune 39
Dillon, Michael 1–2, 5

Diploma, The 41
diplomatic support 41
discrimination 2, 10, 17, 24, 48, 52, 54–56, 68
disease surveillance 3
doctrinal beliefs 6, 10
Durkheim, Émile 6

economy 35; cooperation 41, 42; development 41; expansion 37; integration 36; liberalization 42
ethnic cleansing 11, 16, 48
ethnic conflict 9, 34, 56
ethnic diversity 7
ethnic groups 2, 6, 12, 15, 16, 52, 55, 56, 62, 63, 68
ethnic identity 2, 6, 10, 12–15, 67, 68, 73
ethnicity 12, 16, 52, 53, 56, 57, 66, 67
ethnocentrism 54–57
Europe 54
European Court of Human Rights 6
European Union 5

Falk, Richard A. 26n3
Fleischmann, Klaus 15
foreign policy 34, 36, 47
Fortify Rights report 68
fundamental freedoms 22, 25

Gaffar, Abdul 63, 64
Galagoda Aththe Gsanasara Thero 9
general election: 1956 63, 64; 1990 64–65; 2010 65, 66
Geneva Conventions (1949) 28n43
genocide 4, 5, 16–18, 24, 25, 46, 48, 53, 69
Genocide Convention 26n6
"Geographical Pivot of History, The" (Mackinder) 36
"Geography of Chinese Power, The" (Kaplan) 36
geopolitics 34, 39, 47; concern 48; modern 35; strategies and Rohingya crisis 34–37
Gert Rosenthal Report 48
Gerver, Mollie 4
Goldman Sachs 35
Government of Bangladesh 3, 5, 16, 17, 20, 34, 38, 47

Government of Myanmar 3–5, 4, 11, 13, 14, 16, 18, 19, 23, 24, 36, 38, 43–47, 52, 53, 55, 62, 66, 67, 70–74; response 19–21

Hadi, Abdul 66
Hague Conventions (1907) 21
Haque, Shahidul 12
Hau Do Suan 4, 5
Haviland, Charles 8
"How to Compare Regional Powers: Analytical Concepts and Research Topics" (Nolte) 35
human dignity 2
humanitarian concern 3, 37, 48
humanitarian obligations 16
human rights 1, 3, 4, 6, 9, 11, 16, 17, 22, 25, 55; enforcement 74; violation 16, 18, 20, 42
Human Rights Council 17

Ibrahim, Azeem 15
identity 6–7, 12; Muslim 7; national 9, 55, 57; Rohingya's 66, 67, 74
imaginary geography 2, 25, 26n3
Independent Commission of Enquiry 20
India 34–37, 46, 47; relationship with Myanmar 39–41
India–Myanmar bilateral relationship 36, 37, 40, 41
indigenous ethnicity 67
Indonesia 45
international aid agencies 3
International Convention on the Elimination of All Forms of Racial Discrimination: Article 1 55
International Court of Justice 3
International Criminal Court (ICC) 5, 16, 18–21, 25, 26n6, 27n19, 44
international humanitarian law 11, 16, 20, 24
international justice 21–24
international law 2, 3, 17, 18, 19, 21, 22
International Military Tribunal 21
international system 35, 37
International Tribunal of the Law of Sea Convention (1982) 37
Islam 6, 9, 10, 58, 67
Islam, Nurul 70, 71, 73

Islamic State of Iraq and Syria (ISIS) 4, 58
Islamic terrorists 4
Islamization 8
Islamophobia 54, 58–60, 68

Jamiat-e-Ulema 63
Jerryson, Michael 7, 8
jihād 7, 8, 10
Jilani, A. F. K. 63

Kader, Hossain 59
Kaladan Multi-Modal Transit Transport project 40–41
"Kalar"/"Kala" 55, 74n1
Kalim, Mohammad *see* Ko Ko Linn
Kamein 7
Kaplan, Robert 36
Karadzic, Radovan 56
Kenyatta Appeal Judgment (2011) 18
Keyes, Charles 9
Khair, Haji Abul 63
Kissinger, Henry 35
Kjellen, Rudolf 35
Kleine, Christoph 10, 11
Ko Ko Linn 70, 72
Kuper, Leo 56
Kyaukpyu Special Economic Zone 43
Kyaw Min 70, 71
Kyaw Tint Swe, U 71

land ownership 4
legal remedy 7
Leider, Jacques P. 12, 14, 27n16, 59, 64
Letpadaung mining project 43
liberalism 1
liberty 25
Look East Policy (LEP) 36, 40

MacGregor, Neil 6
Mackinder, Halford 36
Mahayana Buddhism 10, 11
Malaysia 45
maritime boundary dispute (2012) 37, 38
Marshall, Katherine 8
Maungdaw 63, 64
Maung Zarni 8
Mayu Frontier Administration Area 64
Mayu Ray 64
Mayu region 61

Meah, Ezhar 64
Memorandum of Understanding (MOU) 38, 43
metaphysics 10–11
military courts 18
military support 41
Milošević, Slobodan 56
Min Aung Hlaing 53
Ministry of Defense 64
Ministry of the Office of the State Counsellor 19
Mishra, Binoda 46
Mohibullah 72
moral code 11
moral obligations 16
Mumford, Tina 8
Muslim Bengal 61
Muslims 6–10; Arakanese 16, 61, 62; attacks and massacres on 58, 61, 63; birth rate 4; Chinese (*see* Panthays); connection with terrorist groups 58; leaders 63; settled in Rakhine 13–14, 61
Myanmar 4, 6, 7, 10–12, 15, 25, 26n6, 36, 37, 46, 48; attack on Indians 60–61; contemporary 2; economy 42; gas exportation 38; Indian migration to 39, 60; military forces and operations 5, 16, 17, 24, 52, 53, 70, 73; Mongolian invasion of 42; nationalist movement 60; natural resources access to India and China 41, 43, 44; religion in 8; repression of Rohingya refugees 36; support to China 42–43; *see also* Government of Myanmar
Myanmar Oil and Gas Enterprise 43–44
Myanmar Times 41
Myint Thu 71

narrative history 6, 8, 24, 25
national conflict 56
national courts 21
National Democratic Party for Development (NDPD) 65
National Democratic Party for Human Rights (NDPH) 65
national integrity 67, 69, 73, 74
nationalism 9

nationalist Buddhism 11
nationality 54
national law 20, 22
National League for Democracy (NLD) 43, 69
National Museum, Yangon 68
National Registration Card (NRC) 71
Ne Win 52, 56, 57, 64, 66
Nolte, Detlef 35
non-international armed conflicts 18
nonintervention policy 45
non-State armed groups 18
Nu, U 39, 52, 63, 64
Nu-Atlee Agreement (1947) 70

Operation Nagamin 66, 75n13
Organization of Islamic Cooperation (OIC) 3
Organization of the Islamic Conference 14

Panthays 7, 59
Papazoglou, Alexis 1
peacebuilding mission 8
"Personal Field of Application" (Article 2) 23
PetroChina 43
Philippines 45
Pillamarri, Akhilesh 9
political discourse 59
political geography 35
political ideology 8
political issues 38
political parties 69
political process 66
political responsibility 1
political support 44
politics 11; of identity 6, 14, 24; international 35
Popham, Peter 59
Pre-Trial Chamber 19, 27n19
Principles of International Co-operation in the Detection, Arrest, Extradition and Punishment of Persons Guilty of War Crimes and Crimes Against Humanity (1973) 23, 28n42
public health crisis 17
Public International Law and Policy Group (PILPG) 5
pure blood supremacy 57

Pyithu Hluttaw Law No. 4 (1982) 6, 26n12, 52, 57, 66–67, 70

race 54–57
racism 54, 55, 68, 72
radical evil 24, 25
Rahman, Habibur 68
Rakhine Commission Report 68
Rakhine Inquiry Commission (2012) 62, 75n9
Rakhine state 2, 4–6, 8–10, 12, 15, 17, 23, 39, 40, 41, 47, 48, 53, 58, 59, 68, 70, 73; Buddhists in 25; Muslims in 14, 16, 24; Rohingya in 60–66
Ramya, P S. 40
Rarzar, U 7
Rashid, U 63
Razak, Abdul *see* Shwe Maung
realism 35–36
refugees: in Bangladesh 17, 34; crisis 1, 2, 15, 25, 34, 38, 39, 44–48, 52; history 4; shelter for 3
"Refugee Situation on the Western Borders of Burma, The" (Lewa) 27n16
religion 52; anthropology of 9; beliefs 8, 24; convictions 6; identity 9, 55, 62, 67; liberty of 13; violence 1, 10, 13, 62
repatriation 2, 4, 17, 19, 20, 34, 36, 38, 44–47, 69, 71, 72
repatriation agreement (1978) 71
"Report of the Independent International Fact-Finding Mission on Myanmar" 17
Responsibility to Protect (R2P) 48
Rohingya education center, Malaysia 57
Rohingya National Forum 70
Rohingya people 2–4, 6, 12, 14, 48, 53, 65, 74; attacks against 5; as Bengalis 12–15, 55; citizenship status 39; crimes against 18, 25; exclusion 66–67; hatred against 54, 67–69; Muslims 38, 41, 43–45, 52, 53, 56, 57, 59, 61–64, 73; persecution 11, 16, 17, 25, 38, 46, 53, 73; in Rakhine state 60–66; return to Myanmar 44; shelters in Bangladesh *54, 69*; struggle 69–73; women trafficking and rape 5, 17

Rohingyaphobia 58–60
Rohingya Solidarity Organization 13
Rome Statute 16; Article 12(2)(a) 19; Article 19(3) 19, 20
Rosenberg, Alex 6
Runnymede Trust 58
Russia 36, 46, 47; *see also* Soviet Union
Rütland, Anchalee 12

Second World War 21, 24, 62
security forces *see* Tatmadaw
Selth, Andrew 15
Shwe Maung 66
Sittwe port 41
South Asia 2, 9, 48, 61
Southeast Asia 9, 36, 39–42, 48, 61
sovereignty 20, 25
Soviet Union 54; *see also* Russia
Special Economic Zone 37
Special Rapporteur Report 48
spiritual experience 10
Sri Lanka 9
State Law and Order Restoration Council (SLORC) 44, 64
State Peace and Development Council (1997) 44
stigmatization 2
Straits Times, The 59
Students and Youth League for Mayu Development 65
Suez Canal 60
Summer, William G. 56

Tahay, Abu 70, 72
Taninthary 60
Tatmadaw 5, 8, 17, 69, 75n18
territorial dispossession 6
territorial integrity 20, 23
terrorism 4
Thein Sein 53
Theravada Buddhism 9, 11, 61, 62
Third Committee of the UN General Assembly (2018) 3
'three-phase' plan 44
Thura Aung Ko 4

Time 59
trade 39–41
Turkey 3

Ullah, Ata 58
ultranationalism 56
UN Convention Relating to the Status of Refugees 2
UN General Resolution (1992) 24
UN International Law Commission 21
Union Election Commission 65
Union Solidarity and Development Party (USDP) 65, 66, 69
United Nations (UN) 22, 43, 44, 46–48, 53, 71
United Nations General Assembly Resolution on the Elimination of All Forms of Intolerance and of Discrimination Based on Religion and Belief (1981) 28n44
United Nations High Commissioner for Refugees (UNHCR) 26n7, 38
United States 35, 42
UN member states 22
UN Refugee Convention (1951) 45
UN Security Council (UNSC) 4, 5, 17, 19, 20, 44, 47, 73
UN Special Investigation Report 48

vaccinations 3
Volkan, Vamik 56, 57

Wade, Francis 9
Wantanasombt, A. 61–62
war crimes 16–18, 21–25
Weber, Max 55
Western tradition 11
Wirathu, Ashin 58–59

xenophobia 9, 58

Yegar, Moshe 63
Yun Sun 44

Zhengyu Wu 35

For Product Safety Concerns and Information please contact our EU representative GPSR@taylorandfrancis.com
Taylor & Francis Verlag GmbH, Kaufingerstraße 24, 80331 München, Germany

www.ingramcontent.com/pod-product-compliance
Lightning Source LLC
Chambersburg PA
CBHW051759230426
43670CB00012B/2358